VERDURE

Also by Gioietta Vitale

Riso

VERDURE

Simple Recipes
in the
Italian Style

Gioietta Vitale

with Robin Vitetta-Miller

CLARKSON POTTER / PUBLISHERS
NEW YORK

Published by Clarkson Potter/Publishers, New York, New York.
Member of the Crown Publishing Group.

Random House, Inc. New York, Toronto, London, Sydney, Auckland
www.randomhouse.com

CLARKSON N. POTTER, POTTER, and colophon are trademarks of Clarkson N. Potter, Inc.

Printed in the United States of America

Design by Maggie Hinders

Library of Congress Cataloging-in-Publication Data
Vitale, Gioietta.
Verdure : simple recipes in the Italian style / by Gioietta Vitale.—1st ed.
Includes index.
1. Cookery (Vegetables)   2. Cookery, Italian.   I. Title.
TX801.V52   2001
641.6'5—dc21   00-045327

ISBN 0-609-60435-X

10 9 8 7 6 5 4 3 2 1

First Edition

To Nicole, Julia, Sara, Elisa, and Sabina and to all the children of the next generation with love.

Contents

Introduction

THIS BOOK is dedicated entirely to vegetables—all prepared in the style of Northern Italy. The chapters are organized by vegetable for a very good reason. I couldn't possibly count the number of evenings I rushed home to make dinner, opened the refrigerator, and discovered that carrots were my only vegetable. And there were days at the market when I couldn't resist the beautiful produce—gorgeous baby artichokes, plump fresh peas, or juicy ripe tomatoes. Unfortunately, once home I was often unable to find a recipe to inspire me. This book is for those evenings— nights when you need a simple yet delicious recipe for vegetables already in your refrigerator or those you couldn't pass up at the market.

The most important element in Italian cooking is freshness. Whenever possible, the highest quality ingredients should be used. I grew up in Milan, where vegetables were a significant part of my youth. I learned how to pick the finest produce and then prepare it in a way that would respect its unique flavors. When you start with quality ingredients, you need very little to enhance the inherent taste of vegetables. Too many additional ingredients and prolonged cooking times mask the tremendous flavor fresh produce has to offer.

Thanks to global shipments of produce, you can enjoy most vegetables year-round—fresh asparagus in October, red ripe tomatoes in December, and tender baby eggplant in April. However, it's important to remember that some vegetables travel long distances to get to your local market. Additionally, many vegetables remain on produce shelves for extended periods of time. Quality and age significantly impact a vegetable's flavor, texture, and cooking time; therefore, use my suggested cooking times as a guideline, and to ensure the best result, keep an eye on the pot, not on the clock.

During one of my frequent visits to Italy I found myself wandering around the enchanting Umbrian hill towns. Umbria, situated one and one half hours from Rome's Fiumicino International Airport, is reachable by car via the *super strada* north heading toward Florence. This pleasant ride provides views of small medieval towns perched on hilltops, silver-gray olive trees, dark green Roman pines, and contrasting golden sunflower fields.

Food in this region is at its simplest and the methods of cooking focus on producing fresh, clear tastes. The flavor of a dish is built upon the main ingredient, without the use of strong seasonings that would overwhelm the food. The philosophy in this book is *simplicity* and the use of fresh ingredients—the two most important elements of Italian cuisine at its best.

Artichokes

C A R C I O F I

ARTICHOKES ARE THE IMMATURE FLOWER BUDS OF A THISTLE PLANT. THE EDIBLE PORTION—THE VELVETY TEXTURE FOUND AT THE BASE OF EACH LEAF AND THE CENTER OF THE "CONE"—TASTES LIKE A CROSS BETWEEN CELERY AND ASPARAGUS.

THERE ARE SEVERAL VARIETIES OF ARTICHOKE, WITH GREEN GLOBE BEING the most readily available. Baby and regular-size artichokes come from the same plant, but their size is determined by placement on the plant. Baby artichokes grow down among the shady base, where they are shielded from the toughening and growth-enhancing rays of the sun. Since baby artichokes are uniformly tender, the whole vegetable is edible, raw or cooked.

Baby artichokes range in size from that of a walnut to a jumbo egg (size is not an indicator of age; some types are just bigger than others). Larger artichokes vary in size from medium (about 8 ounces), to large (about 10 ounces), to jumbo (about 12 ounces).

Artichokes have several parts worth mentioning. The "choke" is the inedible fuzzy portion in the middle of medium, large, and jumbo artichokes (baby artichokes have no choke). Remove the choke easily by scooping it out with a spoon after the vegetable has been steamed or poached. The terms "heart" and "bottom" are often used interchangeably, but they're actually two different things. The "heart," located in the center of the artichoke, comprises the pale, inner leaves and the firm-fleshed base. The "bottom," or saucer-shaped portion of the artichoke, is free of the choke and leaves and is touted as the most prized portion of the vegetable.

Artichokes are available year-round, but spring is the domestic (California) peak season. Choose artichokes that are firm and heavy for their size, with tight, compact leaves. Color varies from green to purplish red, and some artichokes—exposed to an early frost—may have a yellowish tinge or brown spotting; slight discolorations do not affect quality or taste (in fact, some say frost enhances flavor). Since all artichokes are mature when picked, avoid any that look dry or withered. Fresh artichokes have a rich, meaty flavor with a clean aftertaste, but old artichokes can be dull and tasteless.

Baby artichokes are ideal for eating raw in salads. They can also be marinated, sautéed, and added to soups, sauces, stews, and pot roasts. Medium and large artichokes are perfect for side dishes and light meals. When trimmed and sliced, they can be battered and fried, or added to stir-fries and pasta dishes. Stuffed jumbo artichokes make a complete and satisfying entree. To eat the larger artichokes, pull off a leaf, drag it through your teeth, and discard the portion that doesn't come off easily. The tiniest inner leaves are completely edible.

Artichokes pair well with sharp flavors such as lemon, orange, wine, vinegar, olives, capers, smoked meats such as ham and bacon, garlic, shallots, bay leaves, parsley, sage, tarragon, fennel, and oregano. In Italy, we enjoy dipping the leaves in extra virgin olive oil that's been seasoned with a little salt, pepper, and lemon juice.

To prepare artichokes for cooking, slice off the top 1 inch from each artichoke to remove the thornlike tips. Slice the stem end so it's even with the base (or leave 1 inch of stem, if desired) and pull away any dry or tough outer leaves. To prevent discoloration while you are working, immerse trimmed artichokes in a large bowl of ice water that has the juice of one lemon squeezed into it.

To store fresh artichokes, sprinkle them with a little water, place in perforated plastic bags, and store in the refrigerator crisper for up to one week.

COOKING TIMES
(times vary depending on artichoke size; artichokes are ready to eat when an outer leaf pulls off easily)

BOILING (standing in 3 inches of water) and steaming (over 1 to 2 inches of boiling water): 15 to 20 minutes for baby artichokes, 25 to 40 minutes for medium, large, and jumbo artichokes
MICROWAVING (in ½ inch of water): 6 to 10 minutes (for all sizes)

BOILED ARTICHOKES

CARCIOFI LESSATI

6 medium artichokes (about
  8 ounces each)

1 lemon

8 to 9 tablespoons extra virgin
  olive oil

2½ tablespoons white wine vinegar

Salt and freshly ground black pepper

*The beauty of this recipe lies in its simplicity. These artichokes make
a lovely side dish served with roast beef or baked ham.*

SLICE off the top 1 inch from each artichoke to remove the
thornlike tips. Slice the stem end so it's even with the base
(or leave 1 inch of stem, if desired) and pull away any dry or
tough outer leaves. As you trim them, transfer the artichokes to
a large stockpot with enough water to cover and the juice of the
lemon. Set the pot over medium-high heat and bring to a boil.
Reduce the heat, partially cover, and simmer 20 minutes, until
tender (outer leaves will pull off easily).

Drain, turn artichokes upside down, and let cool slightly.

Meanwhile, in a small bowl, whisk together the oil, vinegar,
and salt and pepper to taste. Place the artichokes in individual,
shallow bowls and serve with olive oil mixture on the side for
dipping the leaves.

Serves 6

FRIED ARTICHOKES

CARCIOFI FRITTI

SLICE off the top 1 inch from each artichoke to remove the thornlike tips. Slice the stem end so it's even with the base (or leave 1 inch of stem, if desired) and pull away any dry or tough outer leaves. Transfer the artichokes to a large bowl of ice water that has the juice of 1 lemon added.

In a medium bowl, whisk the egg whites until frothy. Whisk in the yolks and salt.

Drain the artichokes and cut into four equal wedges (lengthwise). There may be tougher leaves and fuzz in the middle. If necessary, using a spoon, remove the inner core of each artichoke quarter (pale inner leaves) and scrape away the fuzzy middle. Return to the bowl of water and lemon juice.

Place the flour in a shallow dish. Drain artichokes well and pat dry with paper towels. Add artichoke wedges to the flour and turn to coat. Dip the flour-coated artichokes into the egg mixture and let stand 5 minutes (they should become saturated with egg mixture).

Meanwhile, heat the olive oil in a heavy stockpot until a thermometer reads 350° to 375° F. Add the artichokes in two or three batches (to keep oil temperature constant) and fry until golden brown on all sides, about 5 minutes. Remove the artichokes with a slotted spoon and drain on paper toweling. Cut the remaining lemon into wedges. Serve the artichokes hot with lemon wedges on the side.

10 baby artichokes
2 lemons
3 large eggs, separated
1 teaspoon salt
1 cup all-purpose flour
3 cups olive oil

Serves 4

RAW BABY ARTICHOKE SALAD

INSALATA DI CARCIOFI CRUDI

12 baby artichokes

4 lemons

4 tablespoons extra virgin olive oil

1½ teaspoons salt

The baby artichokes in this salad are eaten raw, and they are so delicate and tasty—like the petals on a rose. Serve this delightful salad as a first course or as a side dish with veal scaloppini or sautéed chicken.

SLICE off the top ¼ to ½ inch from one artichoke to remove the thornlike tips, if necessary. Slice the stem end so it's even with the base and pull away any dry or tough outer leaves. Transfer to a large bowl of cold water and add the juice from 1 lemon. This is done to prevent discoloration. Repeat with remaining artichokes.

Drain the artichokes and cut each in half lengthwise. Place halves cut side down on a cutting board and thinly slice lengthwise.

Place the artichoke slices in a large bowl and add the juice from the remaining 3 lemons, olive oil, and salt. Toss to combine. Serve immediately.

Serves 4

Variation
BABY ARTICHOKES
WITH PARMIGIANO-REGGIANO
CARCIOFI FRESCHI CON PARMIGIANO-REGGIANO

TOP artichoke slices with thinly sliced Parmigiano-Reggiano cheese (use a vegetable peeler to obtain thin slices).

ARTICHOKE FRITTATA

FRITTATA DI CARCIOFI

Frittatas are delicious.

SLICE off the top ¼ to ½ inch from each artichoke to remove the thornlike tips, if necessary. Slice the stem end so it's even with the base and pull away any dry or tough outer leaves. Transfer the artichokes to a large bowl, add the juice of 1 lemon, and pour over enough cold water to cover.

In a medium bowl, whisk together eggs, Parmigiano-Reggiano, and salt and pepper to taste. Set aside.

Drain the artichokes and cut in half lengthwise. Place halves cut side down on a cutting board and thinly slice lengthwise.

Heat 2 tablespoons of the oil in a large skillet over medium heat. Add the artichokes and sauté 3 minutes, until golden. Remove the artichokes from the pan with a slotted spoon and dry on paper toweling (keep skillet hot).

In a large bowl, whisk the eggs until frothy. Add artichokes and mix well. Add the remaining 2 tablespoons of oil to the hot skillet. Pour mixture into hot skillet and cook 3 minutes, until almost cooked through to the top. Invert the frittata onto a large plate and slide frittata back into skillet, uncooked side down. Cook over medium heat until cooked through (a wooden pick inserted will come out clean).

Serve hot, room temperature, or chilled with remaining lemon sliced on the side.

12 baby artichokes

2 lemons

6 large eggs

2 tablespoons freshly grated Parmigiano-Reggiano cheese

Salt and freshly ground black pepper

4 tablespoons extra virgin olive oil, divided

Serves 4

Asparagus

ASPARAGI

I N T H E A N C I E N T G R E E K L A N G U A G E , *ASPARAGUS* M E A N T "S H O O T ," A N APPROPRIATE NAME FOR THIS GRASSLIKE MEMBER OF THE LILY FAMILY THAT BURSTS OUT OF THE GROUND IN THE SPRING. THESE SHOOTS, OR ASPARAGUS SPEARS, GROW AT DIFFERENT RATES, SO THEY MUST BE HARVESTED BY HAND—A TIME-CONSUMING PROCESS THAT ALSO SHOOTS UP THE PRICE. IF

the shoots were not picked, they would grow into tall, fernlike shrubs with bright red berries.

Asparagus varieties vary in color from green to purple—or a combination of the two. The spears range in thickness from very thin to almost 1 inch thick at the ends. Very thin asparagus is the youngest and most tender. Also available are cream or off-white shoots; this variety is grown without sunlight in order to prevent photosynthesis, the chemical process that turns vegetables green. Whether green, purple, or white, the taste of fresh asparagus is virtually identical.

Available year-round thanks to shipments from the Southern Hemisphere, asparagus is in peak season in the United States from late February through July. Asparagus season is often thought of as the first sign of spring for those anticipating the warmer months.

When shopping, select crisp, tightly closed, straight spears with fresh-looking cut ends. Avoid limp spears and any that show signs of drying at the ends.

Thin asparagus spears are best steamed, boiled, microwaved, sautéed, and stir-fried. The fleshy spears of thicker asparagus are great for roasting and grilling. To prepare asparagus for cooking, rinse the spears under cold water and snap off any woody ends. Thinner spears may need just a slight trimming of the tough ends; thicker asparagus often benefits from peeling the outer layer off of the bottom few inches. Asparagus has great affinities for butter, olive oil, hollandaise sauce, eggs, sharp cheese, shallots, bay leaves, basil, oregano, tarragon, and sage.

Best used within two days of purchase, asparagus will keep up to five days if stored properly, in a tightly closed paper bag in the refrigerator crisper.

COOKING TIMES
(for crisp-tender asparagus)

BOILING, STEAMING, AND MICROWAVING: 4 to 5 minutes for thin spears, 8 to 10 minutes for thick spears

SAUTÉING AND STIR-FRYING: 6 to 10 minutes (depending on spear size)

ROASTING AT 500° F: 8 to 10 minutes

GRILLING: 5 to 7 minutes, turning frequently

ASPARAGUS SALAD WITH POTATO-ANCHOVY DRESSING

INSALATA DI ASPARAGI CON PATATE CONDITE
CON SALSA DI ACCIUGHE

*2 pounds thin asparagus spears,
woody ends trimmed*

1 large potato, peeled and diced

4 tablespoons extra virgin olive oil

8 whole anchovies, chopped

1/2 cup chopped fresh parsley

4 tablespoons fresh lemon juice

Salt and freshly ground black pepper

An interesting blend of salty anchovies, starchy potato, and fresh sweet asparagus. This side dish pairs perfectly with sautéed or grilled chicken and steak. If desired, you can make the dressing in advance and refrigerate. Reheat in a small saucepan over low heat until warm.

BLANCH the asparagus in a large pot of rapidly boiling water for 2 to 3 minutes, until crisp-tender. Drain and immerse in a large bowl of ice water to prevent further cooking. Drain and set aside.

Cook the potato in a small pot of rapidly boiling water for 10 minutes, until fork-tender. Drain and set aside.

Heat the olive oil in a large skillet over medium heat. Add the anchovies and potato and, using the back of a spoon, mash the two together until blended. Sauté 2 minutes, until hot. Remove from the heat and stir in the parsley and lemon juice. Season to taste with salt and pepper.

To serve, transfer the asparagus to a serving plate and spoon anchovy dressing over top.

Serves 4 to 6

ASPARAGUS MILANESE WITH FRIED EGGS

ASPARAGI ALLA MILANESE CON UOVA FRITTE

This traditional Milanese dish is as popular as risotto alla milanese in my home town of Milano. When I was a child, fresh asparagus was available only in the spring (not year-round as it is today). When asparagus season began, so did the wonderful elements associated with springtime—mild weather, aromatic flowers, the thrilling feeling of nature awakening all around us. Serve this dish with a nice dry wine, such as Pinot Grigio (very cold).

28 to 32 medium asparagus spears (about 2½ pounds), woody ends trimmed

½ cup freshly grated Parmigiano-Reggiano cheese

3 to 4 tablespoons extra virgin olive oil, divided

8 large eggs, divided

Salt and freshly ground black pepper

BLANCH the asparagus in a large pot of rapidly boiling water for 2 to 3 minutes, until crisp-tender. Drain and divide onto four serving plates. Sprinkle the top with Parmigiano-Reggiano and set aside.

Heat 1 tablespoon of the oil in a large skillet over medium heat. Add 2 eggs and cook until the yolks are just cooked through, 3 to 4 minutes, turning halfway through the cooking if desired. Arrange the fried eggs on the Parmigiano-topped asparagus. Repeat with the remaining eggs, adding additional olive oil as necessary. Sprinkle the top with salt and pepper and serve warm.

Serves 4

ASPARAGUS SALAD IN
OLIVE OIL AND LEMON

ASPARAGI IN INSALATA CON
OLIO D'OLIVA E LIMONE

2 pounds thin fresh asparagus,
woody ends trimmed

4 tablespoons extra virgin olive oil

1 lemon

Salt and freshly ground black pepper

BLANCH the asparagus in a large pot of rapidly boiling water
for 2 to 3 minutes, until crisp-tender. Drain and transfer to a
large serving platter.

Meanwhile, in a small bowl, whisk together the olive oil and
the juice from the lemon. Season to taste with salt and pepper.
Spoon the dressing over the asparagus and toss to coat.

Serves 4 to 6

Variation
ASPARAGUS WITH VINAIGRETTE

2½ tablespoons vinegar (red or white
wine)

1 teaspoon Dijon mustard

5 to 6 tablespoons extra virgin olive
oil

Salt and freshly ground black pepper

BLANCH the asparagus as described above.
In a small bowl, whisk together the vinegar and mustard. Gradually add the olive oil and whisk until blended. Season to taste with
salt and pepper. Spoon the dressing over the asparagus and toss to
coat.

BAKED ASPARAGUS WITH BÉCHAMEL

ASPARAGI AL FORNO CON BESCIAMELLA

PREHEAT the oven to 425° F.
Use 1 tablespoon of the butter to grease the bottom and sides of an 11x7-inch baking dish. Set aside.

Blanch the asparagus in a large pot of lightly salted, rapidly boiling water for 2 minutes. Drain and transfer to prepared baking dish. Set aside.

Melt the remaining 4 tablespoons of butter in a medium saucepan over medium-low heat. Add the flour and cook until mixture becomes golden, stirring constantly with a wire whisk. Gradually whisk in 2 cups of the milk and simmer until mixture is smooth and thick, about 3 minutes, stirring constantly with a wire whisk. Whisk in the Parmigiano-Reggiano and egg yolks, and simmer 2 minutes, whisking until smooth, adding more milk if necessary to create a fluid and consistent sauce. Remove from the heat and season to taste with salt and pepper.

Pour the sauce over the asparagus in the baking dish.

Bake 10 minutes, until top is golden. Serve hot.

Serves 4 to 6

5 tablespoons unsalted butter, divided

2 pounds thin asparagus spears, woody ends trimmed

2 tablespoons all-purpose flour

2 to 3 cups milk

1/2 cup freshly grated Parmigiano-Reggiano cheese

3 egg yolks

Salt and freshly ground black pepper

SOUP WITH ASPARAGUS TIPS

MINESTRINA CON PUNTE D'ASPARAGI

2½ quarts beef, chicken, or vegetable
    broth (or 2½ quarts water and
    2 bouillon cubes)

9 asparagus tips

2 tablespoons unsalted butter

Salt

This delicate soup is wonderful for special occasions, yet simple enough for any day. Be sure to check asparagus tips after 12 minutes of cooking— they should be al dente, or slightly firm to the bite.

IN a large stockpot over medium-high heat, bring the broth to a boil. Add the asparagus tips, reduce the heat to medium, and simmer 12 minutes, until crisp-tender.

Remove the pot from the heat, add the butter, and season to taste with salt.

Serve hot.

Serves 4

Beans

FAGIOLI

THERE ARE THREE STAGES IN A BEAN'S LIFE. THE FIRST STAGE IS IN EARLY SUMMER WHEN THE BEAN POD (UP TO ONE WEEK OLD) IS TENDER ENOUGH TO SNAP WHEN FOLDED IN HALF. THESE EDIBLE PODS VARY IN COLOR FROM GREEN TO PURPLE, YELLOW, AND VARIOUS COLORS IN BETWEEN. THE SHAPES VARY, TOO. BEANS CAN BE THIN AND ROUND (French beans or *haricots verts*), flat and thick (Italian Romanos), or long and slender (Asian yard-long beans). Bean pods have notable affinities with butter, nuts (especially almonds, hazelnuts, and cashews), dill, mint, chervil, and parsley. When shopping, select bright pods—green or yellow—with no signs of drying or wilting. Fresh pods will keep up to one week in perforated plastic bags in the refrigerator crisper.

The next stage occurs when the shape of the bean seeds becomes visible through the skin of the pod. At this point, the pods are too tough to eat, but the beans are plump and full of flavor. These fresh "shell beans" are available as lima beans, butter beans, and French flageolets. Other varieties that may be locally available include black-eyed peas, fava beans, cannellini beans, and cranberry beans. Shell beans are best when shelled just before cooking, and they pair exceptionally well with onions, leeks, chives, tomatoes, carrots, celery, marjoram, oregano, sage, parsley, thyme, and bay leaves. Look for plump green pods or bright green shelled beans of uniform color. Avoid pods or shelled beans with discolorations or signs of drying. In the pod, shell beans will keep up to three days in the refrigerator crisper. Shelled beans should be used the same day.

A bean's third stage occurs when it has matured and almost all moisture has evaporated. The pod becomes brittle and dry and snaps open to release the mature beans. These beans are found dried at the market. Dried beans require longer cooking times and are often soaked overnight before using. The age of dried beans affects cooking times—the older the bean,

the longer the cooking time. When shopping, look for shiny beans of uniform size and color. Avoid beans with faded color, an indication of age that may cause uneven cooking. Kept in airtight packaging or in covered jars in a dark, cool, and dry place, dried beans will keep up to six months. Dried beans have wonderful affinities with smoked meats, onions, carrots, celery, bay leaves, thyme, rosemary, parsley, basil, cilantro, vinegar, chili powder, cumin, and rice.

NOTE: *When using canned beans, place them in a sieve and run water over them (to remove salt and other flavors from canning).*

COOKING TIMES
(times vary depending on size and thickness of bean pods and type of shell bean)

Bean pods and shell beans
BOILING, STEAMING, MICROWAVING, SAUTÉING, AND STIR-FRYING: 4 to 8 minutes
(some shell beans may take up to 20 minutes to reach crisp-tender texture)
Dried beans
BOILING: 1 to 2 hours

FRESH BEAN SALAD

INSALATA DI FAGIOLI FRESCHI

COOK the beans in a large pot of rapidly boiling water for 5 to 7 minutes, until crisp-tender. Drain and transfer to a large bowl. Add the onion and set aside.

In a small bowl, whisk together the vinegar, salt, and pepper. Gradually add the oil and whisk until blended. Pour the vinaigrette over the beans and onion and toss to coat. Serve warm or chilled.

Serves 4

1 pound shelled fresh shell beans, such as cranberry beans, cannellini beans, or lima beans

1 small red onion, thinly sliced

2 tablespoons white wine vinegar

1½ teaspoons salt

¼ teaspoon freshly ground black pepper

9 tablespoons olive oil

WARM BEAN SALAD WITH PARSLEY

INSALATA DI FAGIOLI CALDI CON PREZZEMOLO

DRAIN the beans and transfer to a large stockpot. Pour over enough water to cover and set pot over medium-high heat. Bring to a boil, reduce the heat, and simmer until the beans are tender, 1 to 2 hours, adding water to cover as needed.

Drain and transfer the beans to a large bowl. Add the parsley, oil, vinegar, and onion and toss to combine. Season to taste with salt and pepper and serve warm.

Serves 6

3 cups dried beans (any combination of black, cannellini, pink, cranberry, chick-peas, and black-eyed peas), soaked overnight

½ cup fresh parsley leaves, chopped

3 tablespoons olive oil

2 tablespoons balsamic vinegar

1 small red onion, thinly sliced

Salt and freshly ground black pepper

BEANS IN TOMATO SAUCE

FAGIOLI ALLA SALSA DI POMODORO

2 tablespoons olive oil, divided

1 small onion, finely chopped

1 pound fresh plum tomatoes, finely chopped

2 pounds shelled fresh shell beans, such as lima beans or fava beans

3 fresh basil leaves, finely chopped

Salt and freshly ground black pepper

HEAT 1 tablespoon of the olive oil in a large saucepan over medium heat. Add the onion and sauté 5 minutes, until tender. Add the tomatoes and simmer 10 minutes, until tomatoes break down and the sauce thickens.

Meanwhile, blanch the beans in a large pot of rapidly boiling water for 5 to 7 minutes, until crisp-tender. Drain and set aside.

Heat the remaining tablespoon of oil in a large skillet over medium heat. Add the beans and sauté 3 minutes, until golden.

Add the tomato mixture to the beans, stir in the basil, and simmer 1 minute to heat through. Season to taste with salt and pepper and serve hot.

Serves 6 to 8

Variation
PASTA AND BEANS
PASTA E FAGIOLI

6 cups water

1 pound shelled fresh shell beans, such as cranberry beans, cannellini beans, or fava beans

3 cups elbow macaroni

Freshly grated Parmigiano-Reggiano cheese

Extra virgin olive oil

IN a large stockpot over medium-high heat, bring the water to a boil. Add the beans, reduce the heat to medium low, and cook 5 minutes. Increase the heat to medium-high and return to a boil. Add the elbow macaroni and cook until al dente, 10 to 12 minutes. Ladle the beans and liquid into shallow serving bowls and top with cheese. Drizzle the top with olive oil and serve hot.

BASIC COOKED BEANS

FAGIOLI LESSATI

Each cup of dried beans will yield approximately 2½ cups cooked beans.

COVER each cup of dried beans with 3 cups fresh water. Let stand 12 hours to overnight. Drain and transfer beans to a large stockpot.

Pour over enough fresh water to cover and set pot over medium-high heat. Bring to a boil, reduce the heat, and simmer until beans are tender, 1 to 2 hours, adding water to cover as necessary.

Drain, then season to taste with salt and pepper.

Variation
QUICK SOAKING METHOD
(Instead of Soaking Overnight)

BRING a large pot of water to a boil. Add the dried beans and boil 2 minutes. Remove from the heat, cover and let stand 1 hour. Drain, and cook as above.

BEAN SALAD WITH
POTATOES AND PARSLEY

INSALATA DI FAGIOLI CON PATATE E PREZZEMOLO

4 cups mixed dried beans (any combination of pink, cranberry, kidney, or others), soaked overnight

2 medium potatoes (about 1½ pounds total), peeled and cut into 1-inch cubes

1 cup finely chopped fresh parsley

2½ tablespoons extra virgin olive oil

Salt and freshly ground black pepper

DRAIN the beans and transfer to a large stockpot. Pour over enough water to cover and set pot over medium-high heat. Bring to a boil, reduce the heat, and simmer until the beans are tender, 1 to 2 hours, adding water to cover as needed.

Add the potatoes to the simmering liquid and cook 10 minutes, until potatoes are fork-tender.

Drain the beans and potatoes and transfer to a large bowl. Add the parsley, olive oil, and salt and pepper to taste and toss to combine. Serve warm or chilled.

Serves 6 to 8

BLACK BEAN SOUP

ZUPPA DI FAGIOLI

*For a thinner soup, use 8 cups fresh water to the pre-cooked beans
instead of 6. You may also substitute chicken, beef, or vegetable stock for
the water if desired.*

1 pound dried black beans, rinsed
   and picked over to remove debris

2 tablespoons olive oil

2 bay leaves

1 teaspoon salt

½ teaspoon freshly ground black
   pepper

BRING a large pot of water to a boil. Add the beans, return
to a boil, and cook 2 minutes. Remove from the heat, cover,
and let stand 1 hour. Drain the water and return the beans to
the pot. Add the olive oil, bay leaves, and 6 cups fresh water
and bring to a boil. Reduce the heat, partially cover, and simmer
1 hour, until beans are tender. Remove the bay leaves, season
with salt and pepper, and serve hot.

Serves 6

Beets

BARBABIETOLE

ONCE THOUGHT OF AS THE "CRIMSON-COLORED" VEGETABLE, BEETS ARE NOW AVAILABLE IN A VARIETY OF COLORS, INCLUDING GOLD, ORANGE, WHITE, AND CANDY-STRIPED (LIKE A CANDY CANE). SHAPE AND SIZE VARY, TOO—THEY CAN BE PERFECTLY ROUND OR LONG AND SLENDER, AND AS SMALL AS A GUMBALL OR BIGGER THAN A TENNIS BALL.

Although beets are available year-round, peek season is summer through early winter. When shopping, use the green leaves as an indication of freshness and look for small, bright green leaves, with no signs of yellowing or drying. If the leaves and roots look moist and fresh, the beets will be, too. If the leaves and stems have been trimmed, select fresh-looking beets of uniform color, and avoid any that look dry, cracked, or shriveled. Always select firm, small- to medium-size beets—the larger the beet, the more likely it is to be dried out or "woody" in texture. Once home, immediately remove the green tops—they extract moisture from the roots and can dry out the beets.

With up to 8 percent of its weight as sugar, the sweet taste of beets pairs well with meat, poultry, pork, and vegetables. Beets have particular affinities with lemon, orange, vinegar, onions, walnuts, parsley, dill, tarragon, mustard, and caraway seeds. Whole beets can be boiled, steamed, roasted, and baked, and can be served warm or chilled. To prepare beets for cooking, trim the ends and scrub the surface to remove dirt. For maximum flavor in chilled dishes, cook the beets with the skins on (whether boiling, steaming, roasting, or baking). When cool enough to handle, peel away the outer skin and use as directed. Small beets may be served whole, while larger beets are best sliced into wedges, sticks, or rounds. Raw, tender beets may also be grated into salads. The green leaves are an excellent substitute for spinach and chard, both cooked and raw in salads.

COOKING TIMES
(times vary depending on beet size)

BOILING AND STEAMING: 20 to 45 minutes
MICROWAVING: 12 to 18 minutes
BAKING AND ROASTING AT 350° TO 400° F:
45 minutes to 1 hour

STEAMED BEETS

BARBABIETOLE A VAPORE

1 pound fresh beets, peeled and sliced
into ¼-inch-thick slices

Salt and freshly ground black pepper

PLACE a colander or steamer basket in a large stockpot and add 1 to 2 inches of water. Add the beets to the colander and bring the water to a boil. Cover and steam 45 minutes, until fork-tender. Season to taste with salt and pepper and serve warm or chilled.

Variations
BAKED BEETS

PREHEAT the oven to 300° F. Rinse the beets and trim the ends (do not remove skin). Place in a shallow roasting pan and bake 1 hour, until fork-tender. Peel and slice into ¼-inch-thick rounds and season to taste with salt and pepper.

ROASTED BEETS

PREHEAT the oven to 400° F. Rinse the beets and trim the ends (do not remove skin). Place in a shallow roasting pan and roast 45 minutes, until fork-tender. Peel and slice into ¼-inch-thick rounds. Season to taste with salt and pepper.

SALAD BEETS

BARBABIETOLE IN INSALATA

A very simple, cool salad that can be served year-round.

RINSE the beets under cold water, drain, and transfer to a large bowl. Add the parsley, oil, and vinegar and toss to coat. Season to taste with salt and pepper and serve (or refrigerate until ready to serve).

Serves 4

3 cups sliced steamed beets (see page 34) or 2 10-ounce jars sliced beets, drained

1/2 cup chopped fresh parsley

3 tablespoons extra virgin olive oil

1 1/2 tablespoons red wine vinegar

Salt and freshly ground black pepper

SPIRITED BEETS

BARBABIETOLE PICCANTI

This salad must marinate for 2 hours before serving.

RINSE the beets and trim the ends (do not remove skins). Blanch the beets in a large pot of rapidly boiling water for 5 minutes. Drain and cool.

Peel the beets and slice into thin rounds and transfer to a large bowl. Add the onion, parsley, olives, and sugar.

Whisk together the vinegar and oil and season to taste with pepper. Pour the dressing over the beets and toss to combine. Let stand 2 hours before serving (refrigerate if desired).

Serves 4

2 bunches (about 2 pounds) fresh beets

1 medium onion, thinly sliced, rings separated

1/2 cup minced fresh parsley

6 green olives, pitted and halved

1 1/2 tablespoons sugar

1 1/2 cups white wine vinegar

1 1/2 tablespoons olive oil

Freshly ground black pepper

BEETS WITH CREAM

BARBABIETOLE ALLA PANNA

1 pound beets
1½ tablespoons unsalted butter
½ cup heavy cream
Salt

PREHEAT the oven to 300° F.
Rinse the beets and trim the ends (do not remove skins). Transfer the beets to a shallow roasting pan and bake 1 hour, until fork-tender. When cool enough to handle, peel the beets and slice into ¼-inch-thick rounds and set aside.

In a large skillet over medium heat, melt the butter. Add the beets and sauté 2 minutes. Meanwhile, heat the cream in a small skillet over medium heat until bubbles just appear around edges. Season to taste with salt.

Transfer sautéed beets to a large (preferably warm) serving platter and pour over warmed cream. Serve hot.

Serves 4

Broccoli

BROCCOLI

A HEAD OF BROCCOLI IS A PERFECT BOUQUET OF TINY FLOWER BUDS. EACH SMALL GREEN STALK, KNOWN AS A "FLORET," CONTAINS HUNDREDS OF LITTLE BUDS. AS A PROUD MEMBER OF THE MUSTARD AND CABBAGE FAMILY, BROCCOLI HAS A SIMILAR, MILD MUSTARD FLAVOR. THIS WONDERFUL FLAVOR PAIRS EXCEPTIONALLY WELL WITH TOASTED almonds and pine nuts, cream and cheese sauces, butter, olive oil, shallots, small onions, lemons, oranges, vinegar, dill, oregano, parsley, tarragon, and thyme.

Available year-round, broccoli's natural season is late fall through early spring. When shopping, look for dark green heads with tiny, unopened buds. Some varieties may also have a purplish tint, a sign of quality. Avoid limp stalks, florets that are starting to open, and heads with any yellowish tints—all signs that the broccoli is past its flavorful peak. Stored in perforated plastic bags in the refrigerator crisper, fresh broccoli will keep up to three days.

To prepare broccoli for cooking, cut off the florets at the base of their small stalks. Cut larger florets so all florets are about the same size (to ensure even cooking). The stalks are also delicious; just peel away the tough outer skin with a pairing knife, and cut the stalk into 1- to 2-inch pieces. Broccoli florets and stalks can be boiled, steamed, sautéed, and baked. In addition, the fresh green leaves may be used—just cook as you would spinach or chard.

COOKING TIMES
(for crisp-tender broccoli)

SAUTÉING AND BOILING: 2 to 5 minutes
STEAMING AND MICROWAVING: 6 to 8 minutes
BAKING AT 350° F (WITH CREAM OR CHEESE SAUCE): 15 to 20 minutes

BROCCOLI WITH FRESH TOMATO SAUCE

BROCCOLI ALLA SALSA DI POMODORO

If desired, serve the tomato sauce on the side instead of spooning it over broccoli.

4 cups fresh broccoli florets (keep 2 to 3 inches of stalk, discard woody ends)

2 tablespoons olive oil

½ cup finely chopped onion

2 pounds fresh plum tomatoes, chopped

¼ cup fresh basil leaves, finely chopped

¼ cup fresh Italian parsley leaves, finely chopped

Salt and freshly ground black pepper

BLANCH the broccoli in a large pot of rapidly boiling water for 2 minutes, until crisp-tender. Drain, transfer to a shallow serving bowl, and set aside.

Heat the oil in a large skillet over medium heat. Add the onion and sauté 3 to 5 minutes, until golden. Add the tomatoes and simmer 10 to 15 minutes, until tomatoes break down and sauce thickens. Remove from heat and stir in the basil and parsley. Season to taste with salt and pepper. Spoon tomato sauce over broccoli and serve warm.

Serves 4

BROCCOLI SALAD WITH
OLIVE OIL DRESSING

BROCCOLI IN INSALATA CON OLIO D'OLIVA

8 cups fresh broccoli florets (keep 2 to 3 inches of stalk, discard woody ends)

4 tablespoons olive oil

2 tablespoons balsamic vinegar

Salt and freshly ground black pepper

BLANCH the broccoli in a large pot of rapidly boiling water for 2 minutes, until crisp-tender. Drain and transfer to a large bowl. Add the olive oil and balsamic vinegar and toss to coat. Season to taste with salt and pepper and serve warm or chilled.

Serves 6

SPAGHETTI WITH BROCCOLI

SPAGHETTI CON BROCCOLI

4 cups fresh broccoli florets (keep 2 to 3 inches of stalk, discard woody ends)

12 ounces uncooked spaghetti

4 tablespoons olive oil

2 tablespoons chopped fresh rosemary

Salt and freshly ground black pepper

Use a good-quality olive oil for this dish, one with a pure, fruity flavor. I like to pass additional olive oil at the table, for those who prefer more. If desired, also serve this with freshly grated Parmigiano-Reggiano.

BLANCH the broccoli in a large pot of rapidly boiling water for 2 minutes, until crisp-tender. Drain and set aside.

Cook the spaghetti in a large pot of rapidly boiling water until al dente, 10 to 12 minutes. Drain and transfer to a large bowl. Add the broccoli, olive oil, and rosemary and toss to combine. Season to taste with salt and pepper and serve warm.

Serves 4

BROCCOLI IN WHITE WINE

BROCCOLI IN VINO BIANCO

BLANCH the broccoli in a large pot of rapidly boiling water for 1 minute. Drain and set aside.

Heat the oil in a large skillet over medium-high heat. Add the broccoli and sauté 2 minutes, until edges are golden. Add the wine and bay leaves and simmer 5 minutes, until broccoli is crisp-tender. Remove the bay leaves, season to taste with salt and pepper, and serve warm.

4 cups fresh broccoli florets (keep 2 to 3 inches of stalk, discard woody ends)

1 tablespoon olive oil

½ cup dry white wine

2 bay leaves

Salt and freshly ground black pepper

Serves 4

BROCCOLI WITH PARSLEY

BROCCOLI SALTATI CON PREZZEMOLO

A perfect companion for meat and poultry. If your guests are broccoli fans, you may want to increase the number of florets.

16 florets fresh broccoli

1½ tablespoons olive oil

½ cup chopped fresh parsley

Salt and black pepper to taste

BLANCH the broccoli in a large pot of rapidly boiling, lightly salted water for 1 to 2 minutes. Drain and set aside.

Heat the oil in a large nonstick skillet over medium heat. Add the broccoli and sauté 2 minutes. Remove from the heat, add the parsley, and toss to coat. Season to taste with salt and pepper and serve hot.

Serves 4

Carrots

C A R O T E

IN THE VEGETABLE FAMILY, CARROTS ARE SECOND ONLY TO BEETS IN TERMS OF SUGAR CONTENT. AVAILABLE EVERY DAY OF THE YEAR, CARROTS RARELY WAVER IN QUALITY. THE SUMMER AND AUTUMN MONTHS TEND TO HAVE THE FRESHEST CARROTS, BUT WITH SHIPMENTS FROM ALL OVER THE COUNTRY (CALIFORNIA, ARIZONA, TEXAS, AND FLORIDA), IT'S

rare to find consistently "unfresh" vegetables.

When shopping, choose firm, clean carrots with a deep orange color. Avoid greentinted carrots, a sign they may be bitter. And avoid rubbery and shriveled carrots, or vegetables with any small cracks (microorganisms may be hiding in there). The size of each carrot should be no

more than 8 inches long and 2 inches in diameter (larger carrots can be "woody"). Baby or miniature carrots (about 3 inches long) are sweet and wonderful and work in any recipe calling for regular carrots. If green tops are attached, remove them as soon as you get home—they extract moisture from the carrot, causing bitter ness and drying. When buying pre-packaged carrots (in pound bags), peek through the plastic to look for sprouting at the top or wilting at the bottom. Both are signs of age and spoilage. Stored in perforated plastic bags in the refrigerator crisper, carrots will keep up to two weeks.

Not only delicious raw, carrots are suitable for virtually any cooking method—boiling, steaming, baking, roasting, grilling, stir-frying, deep-frying, and stewing. Since carrots become sweeter as they cook, they make perfect flavoring agents for soups and stews. And both regular and baby carrots make great "beds" for chicken, beef, and pork roasts. For a sweet dish, sauté sliced carrots in butter and add brown sugar and raisins or currants. For a refreshing side dish, steam baby carrots and toss them with fresh dill and lemon. Carrots pair well with dozens of ingredients, including peas, potatoes, beef, fish, thyme, parsley, tarragon, curry, oregano, mint, mustard, and nutmeg. Cooking times vary depending on the size of cut carrots (larger pieces take longer to tenderize), but don't fret—carrots are quite forgiving when left alone too long.

SAUTÉED CARROTS

CAROTE SALTATE IN PADELLA

2 tablespoons olive oil

8 carrots, peeled and cut into 2-inch
pieces

2 stems fresh rosemary

1 cup chopped fresh parsley

Salt and freshly ground black pepper

HEAT the oil in a large skillet over medium heat. Add the carrots and rosemary stems and sauté 5 minutes, until carrots are crisp-tender. Add the parsley and toss to coat. Season to taste with salt and pepper and serve hot.

Serves 4

FRIED CARROTS

CAROTE FRITTE

I like to serve this dish with diced hard-boiled eggs sprinkled over top.

8 carrots, peeled and cut julienne
style (matchstick-size pieces)

2 teaspoons salt

1½ cups all-purpose flour

2 egg yolks, lightly beaten

4 tablespoons olive oil

Salt and freshly ground black pepper

IN a large bowl, combine the carrots and salt. Toss to combine and let stand 1 hour.

Place the flour in a shallow dish, add the carrots, and toss to coat. Dip the flour-coated carrots in beaten egg yolk and turn to coat all sides.

Heat the oil in a large skillet over medium-high heat. Add the carrots and sauté 5 to 7 minutes, until golden brown and crisp-tender. Remove the carrots with a slotted spoon and drain on paper toweling. Season to taste with salt and pepper and serve warm.

Serves 4

 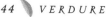

CARROT SALAD

CAROTE IN INSALATA

Grated carrots tend to discolor over time, so prepare this salad just before serving.

U SING a hand grater or the shredder attachment on a food processor, grate the carrots. Transfer to a large bowl and set aside.

In a small bowl, whisk together the olive oil and the juice from both lemons. Pour the mixture over the carrots and toss to coat. Season to taste with salt and pepper and serve.

Serves 4

8 carrots, peeled
2 tablespoons extra virgin olive oil
2 lemons
Salt and freshly ground black pepper

MASHED CARROTS

PUREA DI CAROTE

14 carrots, ends trimmed and peeled, cut into slices

2 tablespoons unsalted butter

Salt and freshly ground black pepper

BLANCH the carrots in a large pot of rapidly boiling, lightly salted water for about 2 minutes, until tender. Drain and transfer to a food processor fitted with the metal blade. Process until finely pureed. Transfer the carrots to a nonstick skillet and set the pan over medium heat. Cook 4 minutes, add the butter, and cook 2 more minutes, until the butter is melted and the mixture is smooth and creamy. Season to taste with salt and pepper. Transfer to a serving bowl and serve hot.

Serves 4 to 6

CARROTS WITH PEAS AND POTATOES

CAROTE, PISELLI E PATATE SALTATE

4 carrots, peeled and cut into small (pea-size) cubes

2 medium potatoes, peeled and cut into small (pea-size) cubes

1½ tablespoons olive oil

2 pounds fresh or thawed frozen peas

Salt and freshly ground black pepper

BLANCH the carrots and potatoes in a large pot of rapidly boiling water for 2 minutes (do not overcook). Drain and set aside.

Heat the oil in a large nonstick skillet over medium heat. Add the carrots, potatoes, and peas and sauté 5 minutes, until potatoes and peas are tender. Season to taste with salt and pepper and serve immediately.

Serves 6

Cauliflower

CAVOLFIORE

THE WORD *CAULIFLOWER* MEANS "CABBAGE FLOWER," AN APPROPRI-ATE NAME FOR THIS BEAUTIFUL MEMBER OF THE CABBAGE FAMILY. CABBAGE GROWS ENCASED IN A LEAF "JACKET," WHICH NOT ONLY PROTECTS THE INNER PORTION FROM THE HOT, DRY SUN (AND SOMETIMES FREEZING NIGHTTIME TEMPERATURES), BUT ALSO PREVENTS THE SUN'S RAYS

from turning this white vegetable green. The green leaves of the jacket are edible, and can be prepared like collard greens.

When shopping, if the green jacket is still attached, look for bright green leaves with a clean white center that leads to the base of the vegetable. Select firm heads with tightly packed, unopened white florets (tiny white bouquets similar to broccoli). Ignore any small gray patches that may appear on the surface—they are an indication that the sun peeked through the leaves (trim that portion off if desired). Stored in perforated plastic bags in the refrigera-tor crisper, cauliflower will keep up to one week.

Milder than its broccoli cousin, cauliflower has similar affinities with mild and sharp cheese sauces, almonds, curry, nutmeg, mustard, peas, and carrots. It is suitable for all types of cooking techniques, including boiling, steaming, micro-waving, baking, sautéing, stir-frying, and deep-frying. Cooking times vary depending on the size of the florets, but as a general rule:

COOKING TIMES
(for crisp-tender cauliflower)

BOILING, SAUTÉING, AND STIR-FRYING: 2 to 6 minutes

STEAMING AND MICROWAVING: 6 to 8 minutes

BAKING AT 350° F (COVERED WITH CREAM OR CHEESE SAUCE): 15 to 20 minutes

CAULIFLOWER SOUP

ZUPPA DI CAVOLFIORE

Lightly sautéed bread cubes add a nice crunch to this creamy white soup, which may be served hot or chilled.

2 tablespoons olive oil, divided

1 small sourdough baguette (about ¼ pound), cut into small cubes

1 head cauliflower, trimmed and broken up into florets

2 cups water or chicken stock

Salt and freshly ground black pepper

HEAT 1 tablespoon of the olive oil in a large skillet over medium heat. Add the bread cubes and sauté 5 minutes, until golden on all sides. Remove from the heat and set aside.

Cook the cauliflower in a large pot of rapidly boiling water for 5 to 7 minutes, until tender. Meanwhile, bring water or chicken stock to a simmer in a saucepan. Drain the cauliflower and transfer to a food processor or blender. With the motor running, gradually add the water or broth and remaining tablespoon of oil and process until smooth. Season to taste with salt and pepper. Serve hot or chilled. To serve, ladle soup into bowls and top with toasted bread cubes.

Serves 4

CAULIFLOWER SALAD

CAVOLFIORE IN INSALATA

1 head cauliflower, trimmed and
    broken up into florets

2 tablespoons extra virgin olive oil

1 tablespoon balsamic vinegar

1 cup chopped fresh parsley

Salt and freshly ground black pepper

COOK cauliflower in a large pot of rapidly boiling water for 5 to 7 minutes, until crisp-tender. Drain and transfer to a large bowl.

In a small bowl, whisk together the olive oil and vinegar. Pour the mixture over the cauliflower, add the parsley, and toss to coat. Season to taste with salt and pepper and serve warm or chilled.

Serves 4

CAULIFLOWER IN BÉCHAMEL SAUCE

CAVOLFIORE AL FORNO CON BESCIAMELLA

PREHEAT the oven to 350° F. Use 1 tablespoon of the butter to coat the bottom and sides of a shallow baking dish. Set aside.

Scald the milk in a small saucepan by heating over medium-low heat until bubbles just appear around the edges. Remove from the heat and set aside.

Melt the remaining 5 tablespoons of butter in a medium saucepan over low heat. Add the flour and cook until the mixture becomes golden brown, stirring constantly with a wire whisk. Gradually whisk in the scalded milk, increase the temperature to medium, and bring the mixture to a simmer, stirring constantly with a wire whisk. Whisk in the Parmigiano-Reggiano and simmer until smooth, stirring constantly with a wire whisk. Season to taste with salt and pepper and remove from the heat.

Meanwhile, blanch the cauliflower in a large pot of rapidly boiling water for 3 minutes, until crisp-tender. Drain and transfer to the prepared baking dish. Pour over béchamel sauce.

Bake 20 minutes, until top is golden. Serve hot.

Serves 4

6 tablespoons unsalted butter, divided

3 cups milk

4 tablespoons all-purpose flour

1 cup freshly grated Parmigiano-Reggiano cheese

Salt and freshly ground black pepper

1 head cauliflower, trimmed and broken up into florets

Celery

SEDANI

A MEMBER OF THE PARSLEY FAMILY, CELERY IS ACTUALLY AVAILABLE IN TWO VARIETIES—WHITE AND GREEN. THE WHITE VARIETY, ALTHOUGH DIFFICULT TO FIND AT THE MARKET, IS OFTEN LABELED AS "BLANCHED," "GOLDEN," OR "GOLDEN HEART." THE GREEN (AND MORE READILY AVAILABLE) VARIETY IS OFTEN LABELED "PASCAL." CELERY IS AVAILABLE

year-round, but prices often rise in autumn and winter months when the domestic crop reduces.

When shopping for celery, use your eyes as your guide. The lightest color with the shiniest surface will have the best flavor (dark green stalks can be stringy). Select well-shaped bunches of celery that are heavy for their size.

The leaves on one end should be moist and bright green and the stalks should be free of cracks, cuts, and bruises. Avoid bunches with darkness at either end, a sure sign of age. Stored in perforated plastic bags in the refrigerator crisper, fresh celery will keep up to one week.

Not just relegated to salads or crudité platters, celery is a wonderful flavoring ingredient for soups, stews, roasts, stir-fries, and sautéed dishes (the leaves add depth to meat, poultry, fish, and vegetable stocks). The pale center stalks, known as the heart, are best served raw, while the outer, greener stalks may be served raw or cooked. Celery will maintain flavor and texture when exposed to long cooking times, such as for soups, stews, and roasts. For a unique side dish, thinly slice stalks and simmer them in a mixture of milk and butter until tender. For a refreshing salad or first course, steam celery stalks over 2 inches of water until crisp-tender, then toss with a vinaigrette and serve warm. Celery pairs well with a variety of ingredients, including mild, sharp, and sweet cheeses; lemon; vinegar; dill; chives; parsley; basil; marjoram; chili powder; cumin; walnuts; pecans; and peanuts.

To prepare celery for eating, separate the stalks and rinse well, making sure to remove any dirt that gathers at the base. Trim the ends and any strings from the outer stalks (use a vegetable peeler for hard-to-remove strings). Celery that has lost crispness (due to long storage) can be "refreshed" by a quick soak in an ice bath.

COOKING TIMES
(times vary depending on size and thickness of slices)

STEAMING AND MICROWAVING: 6 to 8 minutes
BOILING: 1 to 2 minutes
SAUTÉING: 3 to 5 minutes

CELERY WITH GORGONZOLA

Sedani al Gorgonzola

5 ounces gorgonzola cheese, crumbled

2 tablespoons unsalted butter, softened

½ cup fresh parsley leaves, finely chopped

1 head celery, rinsed well, patted dry, and stalks cut into 4-inch-long pieces

Gorgonzola is a classic Italian, blue-veined cheese. You may substitute any variety of blue cheese, if desired. Paired with chilled white wine, this makes a perfect summer appetizer.

IN a medium bowl, combine the gorgonzola, butter, and parsley. Mash together with a fork until well blended. Spoon the mixture into the center of each celery stalk. Cover with plastic and chill until ready to serve.

Serves 4 to 6

CELERY WITH PARMIGIANO, REGGIANO AND BUTTER

Sedani al Burro con Formaggio Parmigiano,Reggiano

8 celery stalks, rinsed well and cut into 2-inch pieces

1 tablespoon unsalted butter

½ cup freshly grated Parmigiano-Reggiano cheese

Salt and freshly ground black pepper

BLANCH the celery in a large pot of rapidly boiling water for 1 minute. Drain and dry completely. Set aside.

Melt the butter in a large skillet over medium heat. Add the celery and sauté 3 to 5 minutes, until golden. Add the Parmigiano,Reggiano and toss to coat. Season to taste with salt and pepper and serve warm.

Serves 4

CELERY SALAD WITH ANCHOVIES

INSALATA DI SEDANI CON ACCIUGHE

PLACE the celery in a large bowl and set aside.
In a small bowl, whisk together the olive oil, vinegar, and
anchovies. Pour the mixture over the celery and toss to coat.
Season to taste with salt and pepper and serve at room temperature or chilled.

Serves 4

*8 celery stalks, rinsed well and cut
    julienne style (matchstick-size
    pieces)*

2 tablespoons extra virgin olive oil

1 tablespoon white wine vinegar

3 whole anchovies, minced

Salt and freshly ground black pepper

SAUTÉED CELERY
WITH BLACK OLIVES

SEDANI SALTATI CON OLIVE NERE

BLANCH the celery in a large pot of rapidly boiling, lightly
salted water for 1 minute. Drain and set aside.
In a large nonstick skillet, heat the oil over medium heat.
Add the celery and sauté 2 minutes. Add water as needed to
prevent sticking and the olives and cook 2 to 3 minutes, or until
the water has almost evaporated. Season to taste with salt and
pepper and serve hot.

Serves 4

*8 celery stalks, cut lengthwise into
    thin vertical slices*

*2 tablespoons olive oil, or more as
    desired*

Up to ½ cup water, if necessary

*5 large black olives, pitted and
    chopped*

Salt and freshly ground black pepper

Cucumber

CETRIOLI

IT'S NO SURPRISE THAT CUCUMBERS ARE MEMBERS OF THE SAME BOTANI-CAL FAMILY AS SUMMER SQUASH (ZUCCHINI AND YELLOW SQUASH). THE FAMILY RESEMBLANCE IS OBVIOUS. WHAT MAY SURPRISE YOU IS THAT CUCUMBERS ALSO SHARE THE FAMILY TREE WITH SWEET MELONS, SUCH AS HONEYDEW AND CRANSHAW. IT BECOMES APPARENT WHEN CUCUMBER PLANTS

and melon vines are placed near each other—it's difficult to tell them apart.

There are basically three varieties of cucumbers available at the market. The small, bumpy-skinned varieties are often used for pickling. The English, European, or Hot House variety is long and thin and often wrapped in plastic. These are semi-seedless and taste better when cooked. The third variety—the dark green, smooth-skinned type—is the most common and certainly the most popular. Unfortunately, this variety is often heavily waxed and must be peeled.

Cucumber season runs from summer to early fall, but thanks to shipments from virtually every state in the union, fresh cucumbers are available year-round. In the winter, when there is a slight drop in production, large shipments are imported from Mexico. When shopping, look for cucumbers that are heavy for their size with a rich, green color. The skin should be firm with no signs of soft spots, bruises, heavy wrinkles, or shriveled ends. Kept in the refrigerator crisper in perforated plastic bags, cucumbers will keep up to one week.

Cucumbers can be eaten raw or cooked, and they have the same cooking properties as their squash cousins. The mild flavor of cucumbers pairs well with sour cream, yogurt, cream cheese, red onions, ripe tomatoes, vinegar, basil, parsley, tarragon, dill, oregano, and mint.

CUCUMBER SALAD

CETRIOLI IN INSALATA

4 cucumbers, peeled and sliced
   crosswise into ¼-inch-thick slices

2 tablespoons red wine vinegar

1½ teaspoons salt

¼ teaspoon freshly ground black
   pepper

½ cup olive oil

3 tablespoons drained capers

*A glass of chilled Chardonnay pairs nicely with this light,
refreshing salad.*

PLACE the cucumbers in a large bowl and set aside.
In a small bowl, whisk together the vinegar, salt, and pepper.
Gradually add the oil and whisk until blended. Pour the mixture
over the cucumbers, add the capers, and toss to coat. Serve at
room temperature or chilled.

Serves 6

SAUTÉED CUCUMBERS

CETRIOLI SALTATI

4 cucumbers, peeled and halved
   lengthwise

2 tablespoons olive oil

½ teaspoon salt

¼ teaspoon freshly ground black
   pepper

USING a small spoon, remove the seeds from the cucumber
halves. Discard the seeds and slice the cucumbers crosswise into ¼-inch-thick slices. Set aside.
Heat the oil in a large skillet over medium-high heat. Add
the cucumber slices and sauté 3 to 5 minutes, until golden.
Add the salt and pepper and toss to coat. Serve warm.

Serves 6

COLD CUCUMBER SOUP

MINESTRA FREDDA DI CETRIOLI

USING a small spoon, remove the seeds from the cucumber halves. Discard the seeds, chop the cucumbers into ½-inch pieces, and transfer the pieces to a blender or food processor fitted with the metal blade. Add the lemon juice and puree until smooth.

Transfer the mixture to a large bowl and stir in the bell pepper. Season to taste with salt and pepper. Cover with plastic and refrigerate 1 hour before serving.

Serves 4

4 cucumbers, peeled and halved lengthwise

½ cup fresh lemon juice

1 red bell pepper, seeded and minced

Salt and freshly ground black pepper

CUCUMBER SALAD WITH TOMATOES AND GREEN OLIVES

INSALATA DI CETRIOLI CON POMODORO E OLIVE VERDI

A very special, cool salad that makes an ideal summer luncheon dish.

PLACE the cucumbers, tomatoes, and olives in a large bowl. Whisk together the olive oil and vinegar and pour over the vegetables. Toss to coat. Season to taste with salt and pepper and serve.

Serves 4

3 to 4 medium cucumbers, ends trimmed and sliced into rounds

3 medium, ripe tomatoes, sliced into rounds

6 green olives, pitted and chopped

2½ tablespoons olive oil

1 tablespoon vinegar

Salt and freshly ground black pepper

Eggplant

MELANZANE

K NOWN AS THE "APPLE OF LOVE," THE EGGPLANT HAS BEEN ADORED ALL OVER THE WORLD FOR CENTURIES. EGGPLANTS WERE NAMED FOR THE SMALL, WHITE, EGG-SHAPED VARIETIES THAT WERE INTRODUCED TO THE ENGLISH DURING THE SEVENTEENTH CENTURY. THE NAME REMAINS TODAY, EVEN FOR THE MORE FAMILIAR (AND POPULAR) PURPLE VARIETIES.

Fresh eggplants are available year-round, but peak season is mid-summer through mid-fall. When shopping, select firm eggplants that have tight skin and are heavy for their size. Look for a fresh green cap and stem end, and avoid soft spots or bruises (a sure sign of age and bitterness). Small to medium eggplants are the youngest and usually the most tender.

Some cooks believe in salting eggplant before using it in order to extract excess water and bitterness. When frying, removing excess water by salting helps prevent the eggplant from absorbing a lot of oil during cooking. Salting is best used for the larger eggplant varieties, and is not a necessary step for small and baby eggplant. To salt eggplant, slice the vegetable crosswise into rounds. Salt both sides of the slices and place them in a colander. Cover the slices with paper toweling and weigh down with some form of weight. After 30 to 60 minutes, remove the weight and paper toweling, wipe off excess salt, and use slices as desired.

The versatile eggplant is hearty enough to withstand a variety of cooking methods, including roasting, baking, sautéing, grilling, and broiling. Eggplant's spongelike flesh absorbs flavors from other ingredients and the vegetable pairs exceptionally well with garlic, onions, tomatoes, olive oil, mild and sharp cheeses, oregano, basil, parsley, rosemary, white pepper, and allspice.

COOKING TIMES
(times vary depending on thickness of slices)

BAKING AND ROASTING AT 350° TO 400° F: 20 to 30 minutes
SAUTÉING, GRILLING, AND BROILING: 3 to 5 minutes per side

EGGPLANT WITH TOMATOES AND CHEESE

MELANZANE AL POMODORO E FORMAGGIO

3 tablespoons unsalted butter, divided

4 small eggplants (about 2 pounds total), peeled and cut crosswise into ¼-inch-thick slices

1½ cups milk

1 cup all-purpose flour

2 large beefsteak tomatoes

3 cups vegetable oil

1 teaspoon salt

4 ounces fontina cheese, grated (½ cup)

½ cup freshly grated Parmigiano-Reggiano cheese

PREHEAT the oven to 350° F. Use 1 tablespoon of the butter to grease an 11x7-inch baking dish. Set aside.

In a shallow dish, soak the eggplant slices in milk for 15 minutes. Remove the eggplant from the milk (reserve milk for later use) and dip slices into the flour, turning to coat both sides. Let stand 10 minutes.

Meanwhile, bring a large pot of water to a boil. Cut large X's on both ends of each tomato. Immerse the tomatoes in boiling water for 15 seconds. Drain and, when cool enough to handle, peel off the outer skin. Slice tomatoes into thin slices and set aside.

Heat the oil in a heavy saucepan until a thermometer reads 350° to 375° F. Add the eggplant slices in batches (to keep oil temperature constant), and fry until golden brown, about 2 minutes per side. Remove the eggplant with a slotted spoon, transfer to paper toweling, and sprinkle with salt.

Layer half of the eggplant in the prepared baking dish. Top with the fontina, half of the tomatoes, and 1 cup of the reserved milk. Cut the remaining 2 tablespoons butter into small pieces and arrange half of the pieces on top of the tomatoes in the baking dish. Top with remaining eggplant, tomato, ½ cup milk, and butter. Sprinkle with Parmigiano-Reggiano.

Bake, uncovered, 20 minutes, until top is golden brown. Serve hot.

Serves 8

EGGPLANT MILANESE

MELANZANE ALLA MILANESE

A vegetarian version of veal scaloppini (cotolette alla milanese).

DIP the eggplant slices into the flour and turn to coat both sides. Shake off excess flour and dip slices into egg and then into bread crumbs, turning to coat both sides.

Heat the oil in a large skillet over medium heat. Add the eggplant slices in batches (to prevent crowding) and sauté 2 to 3 minutes per side, until golden brown. Remove the eggplant with a slotted spoon, transfer to paper toweling, and sprinkle with salt. Serve hot.

Serves 6

4 small eggplants (about 2 pounds total), ends trimmed and cut crosswise into 1/2-inch-thick slices

1 cup all-purpose flour

1 large egg, lightly beaten

2 cups dry bread crumbs

2 tablespoons vegetable oil, or more as needed

1 teaspoon salt

GRILLED EGGPLANT

MELANZANE AI FERRI

PREHEAT the outdoor grill or stove-top grill pan. Brush both sides of the eggplant slices with olive oil and place on hot grill. Cook 3 minutes, flip, and cook 3 more minutes, until golden brown on both sides. Season to taste with salt and pepper and serve hot.

Serves 6

4 small eggplants (about 2 pounds total), cut crosswise into 1/2-inch-thick slices

2 tablespoons olive oil

Salt and freshly ground black pepper

EGGPLANT CROQUETTES

CROCCHETTE DI MELANZANE

6 small eggplants (about 3 pounds total), peeled and cut into 2-inch pieces

3 cups vegetable oil

1 cup fresh basil leaves, finely chopped

1 cup fresh parsley leaves, finely chopped

1 cup freshly grated Parmigiano-Reggiano cheese

2 large eggs, lightly beaten

1 teaspoon salt, divided

1/2 teaspoon freshly ground black pepper

1 cup all-purpose flour

4 to 6 tablespoons olive oil

2 lemons, quartered

BLANCH the eggplant pieces in a large pot of rapidly boiling water for 1 minute. Drain and dry completely on paper toweling (eggplant must be completely dry to prevent oil from splattering when frying).

Heat the vegetable oil in a heavy saucepan until a thermometer reads 350° to 375° F. Add the eggplant pieces in batches (to keep oil temperature constant) and fry 3 to 5 minutes, until golden brown on all sides. Remove the pieces with a slotted spoon and drain on paper toweling. When cool enough to handle, dice the eggplant and transfer to a large bowl. Add the basil, parsley, Parmigiano-Reggiano, eggs, 1/2 teaspoon of the salt, and the pepper and mash together until well blended.

Drop 1/4 cup of the mixture into the flour and gently roll until coated on all sides (while rolling, shape into an oval). Repeat to make 16 croquettes.

Heat 4 tablespoons of the olive oil in a large skillet over medium-high heat. Add the croquettes in batches (to prevent crowding) and sauté 3 to 5 minutes, until golden brown on all sides, adding additional olive oil if necessary to prevent sticking. Remove croquettes with a slotted spatula, transfer to paper toweling, and sprinkle with remaining 1/2 teaspoon salt. Serve hot, with lemon wedges on the side.

SERVES 8

EGGPLANT IN TOMATO SAUCE

MELANZANE AL FORNO CON SALSA DI POMODORO

SPREAD out the eggplant slices on a large baking sheet and sprinkle with salt. Let stand 1 hour.

To make the tomato sauce, heat 2 tablespoons of the oil in a large skillet over medium heat. Add the onion and sauté 3 to 5 minutes, until golden. Add the tomatoes and simmer 10 to 15 minutes, until tomatoes break down and sauce thickens. Remove from the heat and stir in the basil. Season to taste with salt and pepper and set aside.

Use butter to grease the bottom and sides of an 11x7-inch baking dish. Set aside.

Dip the eggplant slices in flour and turn to coat both sides. Heat 1 of the remaining tablespoons of oil in a large skillet over medium-high heat. Add the eggplant slices in batches (to prevent crowding), adding more oil as necessary, and sauté 3 to 5 minutes, until golden brown on both sides. Transfer slices to paper toweling to drain.

Preheat broiler.

Layer the eggplant slices in the bottom of the prepared baking dish. Pour over tomato sauce. In a medium bowl, whisk together the eggs, Parmigiano-Reggiano, and bread crumbs. Spoon mixture evenly over the tomato sauce. Top with chopped parsley.

Broil 3 to 5 minutes, until top is golden brown and bubbly. Serve hot.

Serves 8

6 small eggplants (about 3 pounds total), peeled and cut crosswise into ¼-inch-thick slices

2 teaspoons salt

4 tablespoons olive oil, divided

½ cup finely chopped onion

2 pounds fresh plum tomatoes, chopped

¼ cup fresh basil leaves, finely chopped

Salt and freshly ground black pepper

1 tablespoon unsalted butter

1 cup all-purpose flour

2 large eggs, lightly beaten

1 cup freshly grated Parmigiano-Reggiano cheese

3 tablespoons dry bread crumbs

1 cup fresh parsley leaves, finely chopped

Fennel

FINOCCHI

FENNEL IS NATIVE TO THE MEDITERRANEAN AND HAS BEEN A FAVORITE IN ITALY SINCE ANCIENT TIMES. ROMANS USED FENNEL TO SEASON MEATS, SEAFOOD, AND A VARIETY OF SAUCES. TRADITIONALLY, ITALIANS SERVE FENNEL AT ANY POINT IN THE MEAL, FROM APPETIZERS THROUGH DESSERT.

Fennel is most prized for its enlarged base, known as the bulb. Extending out from the bulb are celerylike stalks and fernlike leaves. Both the bulb and stalks are delightful raw, served with dips and light sauces, or tossed into salads. Fennel's slightly sweet, licorice flavor adds a unique twist to a variety of dishes, including meat and vegetable stir-fries, grilled fish and chicken, braised beef and pork roasts, vegetable soups, and hearty meat stews. The stalks and slices of the bulb can be batter-dipped and fried, or topped with bread crumbs and Parmigiano-Reggiano cheese and broiled until golden. Fennel's other affinities include tomatoes, oranges, lemons, apples, walnuts and pecans, mild and sweet cheeses, dill, and marjoram. And, traditional Italian meals are often completed with a fresh stalk of fennel to cleanse the palate.

Fennel is available year-round, with peak season running September through May. When shopping, select firm white bulbs with crisp, bright greens. Avoid soft bulbs and any indication of cracking, dark patches, or bruises. Stored in perforated plastic bags in the refrigerator crisper, the stalks will keep up to four days, the bulbs for up to one week.

To prepare fennel for serving raw or cooked, slice the bulb from the stalks. Trim the bulb's root end and slice bulb as desired. If cutting bulb in advance, brush with a little lemon juice to prevent discoloration. Trim the dry ends of fennel stalks, rinse stalks well to remove any dirt, and use as desired. The feathery leaves can be chopped and used as an herb or decorative garnish.

COOKING TIMES

SAUTÉING, STIR-FRYING, AND DEEP-FRYING: 3 to 5 minutes

BLANCHING AND BOILING: 4 to 6 minutes

BAKING AND ROASTING AT 350° TO 400° F: 30 minutes (both the bulb and stalks of fresh fennel are suitable for long cooking times)

FENNEL SALAD

FINOCCHI IN INSALATA

2 whole fennel bulbs with stalks
2 tablespoons olive oil
2 lemons
Salt and freshly ground black pepper

The perfect addition to a summer luncheon of cold cuts, cheese, and fresh fruit.

TRIM the ends and tops from the fennel and separate into stalks. Rinse thoroughly to remove dirt and slice the stalks into thin, 2-inch-long slices. Transfer to a large bowl and add the olive oil and the juice from both lemons. Season to taste with salt and pepper.

Refrigerate until ready to serve.

Serves 4 to 6

SAUTÉED FENNEL WITH PARMIGIANO-REGGIANO

FINOCCHI SALTATI AL PARMIGIANO-REGGIANO

4 whole fennel bulbs, ends and stalks trimmed, bulbs thinly sliced
3 tablespoons olive oil
½ cup freshly grated Parmigiano-Reggiano cheese
Salt and freshly ground black pepper

BLANCH the fennel in a large pot of rapidly boiling water for 2 minutes. Drain and set aside.

Heat the oil in a large nonstick skillet over medium heat. Add the fennel and sauté 3 to 4 minutes, until golden. Remove from the heat, add the Parmigiano-Reggiano, season to taste with salt and pepper, and toss to combine. Serve hot.

Serves 4 to 6

BAKED FENNEL
WITH BÉCHAMEL SAUCE

An excellent partner for roast chicken.

BLANCH the fennel in a large pot of rapidly boiling water for 3 minutes. Drain and set aside.

Heat the oil in a large skillet over medium-high heat. Add fennel slices in batches (to prevent crowding) and sauté 3 to 5 minutes, until golden. Remove the slices with a slotted spoon and transfer to a shallow baking dish. Set aside.

Preheat the broiler.

Scald the milk in a small saucepan by heating over medium-low heat until bubbles just appear around the edges. Set aside.

Melt the butter in a small saucepan over low heat. Add the flour and cook until the mixture becomes golden brown, stirring constantly with a wire whisk. Just as the mixture turns golden, it will become very stiff, which is just right. Gradually whisk in scalded milk, increase the temperature to medium, and bring the mixture to a simmer, whisking constantly (ignore any small lumps). Whisk in the cheese and whisk until smooth. Season to taste with salt and pepper and pour over the fennel in the baking dish.

Broil 3 to 5 minutes, until top is golden and bubbly. Serve hot.

Serves 8

4 whole fennel bulbs with stalks, ends and stalks trimmed, bulbs thinly sliced

3 tablespoons olive oil

2 cups milk

3 tablespoons unsalted butter

3 tablespoons all-purpose flour

½ cup freshly grated Parmigiano-Reggiano cheese

Salt and freshly ground black pepper

FENNEL WITH BRESAOLA

FINOCCHI ALLA BRESAOLA

24 thin slices bresaola (about
  12 ounces total)

2 whole fennel bulbs, ends and stalks
  trimmed, bulbs thinly sliced

2 tablespoons olive oil

1 lemon

½ teaspoon salt

Bresaola is boneless air-dried beef that is frequently served on an affettato (assorted cured-meat platter), and its distinct taste pairs nicely with sweet, anise-flavored fennel. This dish is a year-round delight that I often serve with a crouton-topped, vegetable consommé. For a complete meal, serve lemon sorbet and mixed fruit salad for dessert.

ARRANGE the bresaola in the bottom of a shallow serving dish, allowing slices to overlap slightly. Top with fennel slices.

In a small bowl, whisk together the olive oil, the juice from the lemon, and the salt. Pour the mixture over the fennel and bresaola. Serve immediately or cover with plastic and refrigerate until ready to serve (up to 4 hours).

Serves 4 to 6

Lentils

LENTICCHIE

IN MY HOMETOWN OF MILANO, LENTILS ARE SYNONYMOUS WITH MONEY. THAT'S WHY ON EVERY MENU FOR THE MILANESE NEW YEAR'S EVE DINNER LENTILS ARE INCLUDED TO ASSURE PROSPERITY IN THE YEAR TO COME. THE LENTIL IS PROBABLY THE OLDEST CULTIVATED LEGUME. ITS LATIN NAME, *LENS*, IS THE WORD WE NOW USE FOR DOME-SHAPED GLASS.

Lentils are thin-skinned and require no soaking before cooking. The olive-colored variety, often called "green," is the most widely available. Green lentils cook rather quickly (15 to 30 minutes) and they end up with a soft texture and mild taste. They can be used in soups and stews, as a base for stir-fries and sautéed dishes, or served alone tossed with olive oil and parsley.

French lentils are much darker green and about half the size of green lentils. The cooking time is the same, but since French lentils remain firm after cooking, they make the better choice for salads. They pair exceptionally well with olive and nut oils, parsley, basil, bay leaves, vinegar, wine, red onions, tomatoes, carrots, celery, spinach, and olives.

There are other kinds of lentils, such as red, yellow, or beluga, which have shorter cooking times, and which in the case of the red and yellow become very mushy when cooked. The Italians use primarily the green lentils and sometimes the smaller French kind.

LENTIL SALAD

LENTICCHIE IN INSALATA

PLACE the lentils in a large stockpot and pour over enough water to cover. Bring to a boil, reduce the heat, and simmer 15 to 30 minutes, until lentils are tender.

Drain the lentils and transfer to a large bowl. Add the parsley, olive oil, and vinegar and toss to combine. Season to taste with salt and pepper and serve warm or chilled.

Serves 4

2 cups green lentils, rinsed and picked over to remove debris

½ cup chopped fresh parsley

4 tablespoons olive oil

2 tablespoons balsamic vinegar

Salt and freshly ground black pepper

LENTILS WITH PANCETTA

LENTICCHIE CON PANCETTA

A perfect partner for cotechino (pork sausage made with garlic and spices) or any beef dish.

IN a large stockpot, combine the lentils, water, pancetta, onion, and sage. Set the pan over medium-high heat and bring the mixture to a boil. Reduce the heat to medium-low and simmer 45 minutes to 1 hour, until lentils are tender and the liquid is absorbed. Season to taste with salt and pepper.

Serves 4

½ pound green lentils, rinsed and picked over to remove debris

4 cups water

4 ounces pancetta, diced

1 small onion, chopped

2 sage leaves, minced

Salt and freshly ground black pepper

 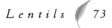

LENTIL SOUP

MINESTRINA DI LENTICCHIE

*1 pound green lentils, rinsed and
picked over to remove debris*

*8 cups chicken or beef stock, or more
as desired.*

2 bay leaves

Salt and freshly ground black pepper

*The list of ingredients may seem short, but that's the beauty of this
recipe—simple and delightful. For a thinner soup, add additional stock as
desired. You may also serve freshly grated Parmigiano-Reggiano cheese on
the side. Use a vegetable peeler on a block of Parmigiano-Reggiano and
arrange the curls on top of soup just before serving.*

COMBINE the lentils, stock, and bay leaves in a large stockpot. Set the pot over medium-high heat and bring the
mixture to a boil. Reduce the heat, partially cover, and simmer
30 minutes, until lentils are tender.

Remove the bay leaves, season to taste with salt and pepper,
and serve hot.

Serves 6

LENTILS WITH MIXED VEGETABLES

LENTICCHIE CON VERDURA MISTA

PLACE the lentils in a large stockpot and pour over enough water to cover. Bring to a boil, reduce the heat, and simmer 15 to 30 minutes, until lentils are tender. Drain and set aside.

Heat the oil and butter together in a large skillet over medium heat. Add the tomatoes, carrots, celery, and onion and sauté 8 minutes, until vegetables are tender and tomatoes are broken down. Add the lentils and simmer 1 minute to heat through. Remove from the heat and add the parsley. Season to taste with salt and pepper and serve warm or chilled.

Serves 6

1 pound green lentils, rinsed and picked over to remove debris
3 tablespoons olive oil
2 tablespoons unsalted butter
2 large beefsteak tomatoes, chopped
2 carrots, peeled and chopped
2 celery stalks, chopped
1 medium onion, chopped
1/2 cup chopped fresh parsley
Salt and freshly ground black pepper

Mushrooms

FUNGHI

MORE THAN TWO THOUSAND VARIETIES OF MUSHROOMS ARE EATEN WORLDWIDE—A PHENOMENON THAT'S BEEN GOING ON FOR MORE THAN TWO THOUSAND YEARS. MUSHROOMS AREN'T VEGETABLES; THEY ARE SPECIES OF FUNGI (ALONG WITH TRUFFLES, BREAD MOLD, AND YEAST). IN THE EARLY DAYS, MUSHROOMS WERE FARMED IN

caves, where they would thrive in the cool temperatures. Back then, late fall, winter, and early spring were peak season because the cold climate was ideal. Today, man-made "mushroom houses" that supply a constant flow of cool air make mushrooms available year-round.

White button or commercial mushrooms are the most common, and probably the most popular. They range in size from less than 1 inch to over 3 inches in diameter. Wild mushrooms are available in so many different varieties, you could dedicate an entire book to them. The most popular in Italian cooking, and widely available, are:

- *Porcini* or *boletes*. Like large, red-tinted button mushrooms with thick stalks. They are the most flavorful of all wild mushrooms and their peak season is late spring and fall.
- *Chanterelles* or *girolles*. Deep golden or orange-brown and shaped like a daisy or curving trumpet. The flavor is sweet and earthy with a hint of apricots. *Black trumpets* are similarly shaped and have a similar taste. Peak season for both varieties is summer through winter.
- *Creminis* or *Italian browns*. The same as button mushrooms, just bigger and grown outdoors. The caps are light brown and they have a more mature flavor than the button variety.
- *Portobellos*. Full-grown cremini mushrooms. They can be up to 6 to 8 inches wide and they have a meaty, earthy flavor. Because of their large size, they are perfectly suited for grilling and broiling.
- *Morels*. Small and spongelike. They have a porous surface that is ideal for soaking up rich broths and flavorful sauces. The honey-comblike surface also traps sand, so be sure to plunge them in water before using.
- *Shiitakes*. Umbrella-shaped, these have a woodsy, oaklike flavor and the caps can be eaten raw or cooked. The stems make an excellent flavoring ingredient in soup stocks and stews (discard stems before serving).

Dried mushrooms add intense mushroom flavor to soups, stews, and sauces. Before using, soak dried mushrooms in warm water for at least 15 minutes. Rinse well and remove hard stems before slicing and adding to simmering liquid.

All mushroom varieties pair well with cream, garlic, shallots, pearl onions, mild and sharp cheeses, chicken, beef, veal, firm-fleshed fish (such as tuna and swordfish), peas, rice, barley, sherry wine, tarragon, sage, parsley, thyme, oregano, and bay leaves.

When shopping, choose mushrooms based on your needs. Mushrooms that will be eaten raw should have tightly closed caps. Mushrooms that will be cooked can be a bit older, meaning the caps will be slightly open, revealing the gills. Older or "mature" mushrooms will have a stronger flavor, and because they contain less moisture, they cook more easily. Whatever type you buy, look for firm, dry mushrooms—without dark or soft spots or damp or shriveled caps or stems. Avoid slimy mushrooms, a sign of age and breakdown of texture.

To prepare mushrooms, clean the surface of the cap with a damp cloth or soft brush. Rinse hard-to-clean mushrooms quickly under running water to remove excess dirt. Never soak mushrooms—they absorb water and become mushy. Mushrooms are suitable for a variety of cooking methods, including sautéing, stir-frying, grilling, and broiling. When adding to soups and stews, it is best to brown mushrooms first in butter or olive oil, to bring out the flavor and eliminate any "raw" taste.

Although best used right away, mushrooms will keep up to three days in the refrigerator crisper. For best results, store mushrooms in paper bags (plastic bags may drop moisture back onto the mushrooms).

MUSHROOMS WITH PARSLEY

FUNGHI TRIFOLATI CON PREZZEMOLO

Serve alongside steak or poultry, or spoon over fluffy white rice.

I N a medium bowl, combine the porcini mushrooms and warm water. Let stand 20 minutes. Drain the mushrooms through a fine sieve, reserving ½ cup of the soaking liquid, and rinse off any remaining dirt. Roughly chop and set aside.

Heat the oil in a large skillet over medium heat. Add the cremini mushrooms and sauté 5 minutes, until mushrooms are tender and releasing juice. Add the porcini mushrooms, reserved soaking liquid, and wine, and simmer 5 to 7 minutes, until liquid reduces by half. Remove from the heat and stir in the parsley. Season to taste with salt and pepper and serve hot.

Serves 4 to 6

4 ounces dried porcini mushrooms

2 cups warm water

3 tablespoons olive oil

1 pound fresh cremini mushrooms, stems trimmed and thinly sliced

1 cup dry white wine

1 cup chopped fresh parsley

Salt and freshly ground black pepper

FRIED MUSHROOMS

FUNGHI FRITTI

16 fresh porcini or shiitake
    mushrooms, stems removed, caps
    wiped well

1 cup all-purpose flour

6 to 7 tablespoons olive oil

Salt and freshly ground black pepper

2 lemons, quartered

CUT the mushroom caps into ½-inch-thick slices. Place the flour in a medium bowl, add the mushroom slices, and toss to coat.

Heat the oil in a large skillet over medium-high heat. Add the mushroom slices in two batches (to prevent crowding) and fry 3 to 5 minutes, until golden. Remove mushrooms with a slotted spoon, transfer to paper toweling, and sprinkle with salt and pepper to taste. Serve with lemon quarters on the side.

Serves 4

WHITE MUSHROOMS IN CREAM

FUNGHI COMMERCIALI CON PANNA

1 pound cremini mushrooms

1½ tablespoons olive oil

½ cup heavy cream or half-and-half

Salt and freshly ground black pepper

This dish is excellent with white rice, mashed potatoes, or chicken.

WASH the mushrooms gently, trim the stems, and thinly slice. Set aside.

Heat the oil in a large nonstick skillet over medium heat. Add the mushrooms and sauté 5 minutes, until tender. Add the cream and cook 2 minutes. Season to taste with salt and pepper. Simmer until mixture thickens, about 2 more minutes. Serve hot.

Serves 4

MUSHROOM SAUCE

SALSA DI FUNGHI

Use this delicious sauce to top cooked spaghetti, boiled rice,
or mashed potatoes.

SOAK the dried mushrooms in 1 cup warm water for 10 minutes. Drain and finely chop. Set aside.

Heat the butter and oil together in a large skillet over medium heat. Add the onion and carrot and sauté 2 minutes. Add the flour and stir to coat. Add the veal and chopped mushrooms and sauté 3 minutes. Add the wine and reduce heat to low. Add the crushed tomatoes and 2 tablespoons water. Season to taste with salt and pepper. Cover and simmer 10 to 15 minutes. Serve warm.

Serves 6

3 ounces dried mushrooms

4 tablespoons unsalted butter

2 tablespoons olive oil

1 medium onion, finely chopped

1 small carrot, peeled and finely chopped

2 tablespoons all-purpose flour

¼ pound lean veal, finely chopped

¼ cup dry white wine

1 15-ounce can crushed tomatoes in thick puree

2 tablespoons water

Salt and freshly ground black pepper

RISOTTO WITH PORCINI AND
CREMINI MUSHROOMS

RISOTTO CON FUNGHI PORCINI E CREMINI

1½ ounces dried porcini
mushrooms, or 1 pound sliced
fresh porcini mushrooms, stems
removed, caps wiped well

5 cups chicken broth

2½ tablespoons olive oil

1 medium onion, minced

2 cups arborio (Italian short-grain)
rice

½ pound fresh cremini mushrooms,
stems trimmed and sliced

2 tablespoons unsalted butter
(optional)

3 tablespoons freshly grated
Parmigiano-Reggiano cheese

Salt and freshly ground black pepper

IF you are using dried porcini mushrooms, soak them in
enough hot water to cover for at least 30 minutes. Drain the
mushrooms and rinse well to remove all sand and dirt. Squeeze
mushrooms to remove excess water, chop roughly, and set aside.

Place the broth in a covered saucepan over high heat. When
broth is hot but not yet simmering, reduce heat to low.

Heat the olive oil in a large Dutch oven over medium heat.
Add the onion and sauté gently until golden, about 3 minutes.
Add the rice and stir with a wooden spoon 1 to 2 minutes, until
rice is well coated with oil. Add the fresh cremini mushrooms
and fresh porcini, if using, and sauté for 2 minutes.

Increase the heat to medium-high and add 1 cup of the hot
broth, stirring constantly. When rice has absorbed most of the
liquid, add another 1 cup broth and continue stirring. Repeat
this process as necessary.

After 10 minutes, add the dried porcini, if using. Continue
adding broth and stirring until rice is al dente, or firm to the
bite, about 8 more minutes.

Remove risotto from the heat and stir in the butter, if
desired, and Parmigiano-Reggiano cheese. Season to taste with
salt and pepper and serve immediately.

Serves 4

Onions

CIPOLLE

ECAUSE OF ITS ROUND SHAPE, THE ONION WAS ONCE CONSIDERED A SYMBOL OF ETERNITY AND OF THE UNIVERSE. WHEN I WAS YOUNG, I WAS TOLD THE TEARS CAUSED BY CHOPPING ONIONS WOULD MAKE YOU "SPARKLING BEAUTIFUL." (IF YOU ARE ALREADY BEAUTIFUL AND WANT TO PREVENT TEARING, PEEL ONIONS UNDER RUNNING WATER, OR RUB

a little vinegar on your cutting board.)

Onions vary in size and shape, with the round varieties boasting the strongest flavor—a quality that makes them ideal for cooking. Round onions can be yellow, white, or red. The small onions, often labeled "pearl," are harvested before reaching full maturity. They can be of any variety, therefore pearl onions can be red, white, or yellow. Green onions have green tops and white bottoms and are often referred to as scallions. They have a fresh, mild onion flavor and are best used raw in salads or added to soups, stews, and stir-fries just before serving. Both round and green onions are available year-round.

Sweet onions are grown during the winter in warm climates. These moist, sweet varieties are best used raw in sandwiches and salads and are often labeled Vidalia, Bermuda, Grano, Granexe, and Maui. The round red and Spanish onions are sweeter than the round whites and yellows, and can also be used raw. Owing to their sugar content, sweet onions caramelize beautifully when sautéed with butter or olive oil and a little sugar. Although sweet onions are available year-round, peak season is spring through early summer.

Shallots are small, rusty brown onions that grow in cloves, just like their garlic cousins. They are also available year-round, but peak season for fresh shallots is July through October.

When shopping for any variety, look for firm onions with no soft spots, dampness on the ends, or signs of sprouting. The skin should be dry and easy to peel.

Sweet and green onions are more perishable than the dried varieties. Store them both in perforated plastic bags in the refrigerator crisper for up to one week. Since the round yellow, white, red, and pearl onions are dried, they will last longer—up to one month, in a dark, cool, dry place.

Onions are suitable for virtually all cooking methods, including baking, roasting, grilling, broiling, stir-frying, sautéing, and microwaving. Cooking times vary depending on onion type, whether they are whole or sliced, and the age of the onion. All onions have natural affinities with sugar, olive oil, cream, potatoes, peas, mild and sharp cheeses, cucumbers, walnuts, pecans, almonds, oranges, grapefruit, tomatoes, basil, dill, thyme, oregano, sage, mint, parsley, and caraway.

ONION FRITTATA

FRITTATINA DI CIPOLLE

*Delicious warm or cold, this ideal luncheon dish pairs well with
cold roasted chicken and mixed fresh greens.*

I N a large bowl, whisk together the eggs, milk, Parmigiano-
Reggiano, salt, and pepper. Set aside.

Heat 2 tablespoons of oil in a large skillet over medium heat.
Add the onions and sauté 5 minutes, until golden.

Add the onions to the egg mixture and gently stir to mix
with a whisk. Heat the remaining 2 tablespoons of olive oil in a
nonstick pan over medium heat. Add the egg onion mixture and
cook 3 minutes, until the bottom is set and the eggs are almost
cooked through to the top. Invert the frittata onto a large plate
and slide frittata back into skillet, uncooked side down. Place
skillet over medium heat and cook 1 minute, until cooked
through (a wooden pick inserted near the center will come
out clean).

Serve hot or chilled.

Serves 4

8 large eggs

3 tablespoons milk

1 cup freshly grated Parmigiano-
Reggiano cheese

1 teaspoon salt

¼ teaspoon freshly ground black
pepper

4 tablespoons olive oil

2 medium yellow onions, thinly
sliced

BAKED RED ONIONS

CIPOLLE ROSSE AL FORNO

2 tablespoons olive oil

4 large red onions (about 3 pounds total), ends trimmed

1 tablespoon balsamic vinegar

1 teaspoon salt

I like to serve this as a first course, followed by smoked salmon and sliced, boiled potatoes.

PREHEAT the oven to 300° F.
Use the oil to coat the bottom of a shallow roasting pan. Place the onions in the prepared pan and bake 40 minutes, until tender.

Remove from oven and sprinkle with the balsamic vinegar and salt. Serve hot.

Serves 6

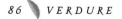

SWEET-AND-SOUR SMALL ONIONS

CIPOLLINE ALL'AGRODOLCE

This rich dish pairs well with a variety of hearty roasts, such as pork, veal, and beef. Serve with a light tomato salad on the side for a complete meal.

1½ pounds small white onions
1 tablespoon unsalted butter
5 tablespoons sugar
1½ tablespoons all-purpose flour
1 cup water
1 cup white wine vinegar

BLANCH the onions in a large pot of rapidly boiling water for 2 minutes. Drain, remove and discard the outer skins, and set onions aside.

Melt the butter in a large skillet over medium heat. Add the sugar and flour and cook until the sugar dissolves and the flour is blended and smooth, stirring constantly with a wire whisk. Add the water and vinegar and bring the mixture to a boil. Reduce the heat and simmer 3 to 5 minutes, until mixture thickens. Add the onions and simmer 2 minutes to heat through. Serve hot.

Serves 4 to 6

BAKED ONIONS

CIPOLLE GRATINATE AL FORNO

2 tablespoons unsalted butter, melted, divided

4 medium onions (about 2 pounds total), peeled

½ cup milk

½ cup freshly grated Parmigiano-Reggiano cheese

Salt and freshly ground black pepper

PREHEAT the oven to 350° F.

Use 1 tablespoon of the butter to grease the bottom and sides of an 11x7-inch baking dish. Set aside.

Blanch the onions in a large pot of rapidly boiling water for 2 minutes. Drain and when cool enough to handle, slice into ¼-inch-thick slices. Transfer the slices to the prepared baking dish and set aside.

In a small bowl, whisk together the milk, cheese, and remaining tablespoon of melted butter. Pour the mixture over the onions and sprinkle the top with salt and pepper.

Bake 20 minutes, until top is golden and bubbly. Serve hot.

Serves 6

Peas

PISELLI

PEAS ARE MEMBERS OF THE LEGUME FAMILY, THE THIRD LARGEST FAMILY AMONG THE FLOWERING PLANTS (AFTER THE ORCHID AND DAISY FAMILIES). THIS FOOD GROUP WAS SO HIGHLY REGARDED IN ANCIENT ROME THAT LEGUMES WERE USED TO NAME FOUR PROMINENT ROMAN FAMILIES—FABIUS FROM THE FABA OR FAVA BEAN; LENTULUS FROM the lentil; Cicero from the chick-pea; and Piso from the pea.

Fresh peas are meaty, rich, and wonderful. Considered by many as the "first sign of spring," peas typically have a peak season from March through early summer. When shopping, select medium-size, bright green pods that are moist and firm, and filled end-to-end with fat peas. Avoid any pods with blemishes or puffed-out areas. For the best results, store fresh peas in their pods and shell them just before cooking. Kept in perforated plastic bags, peas (in pods) will keep up to one week in the refrigerator crisper. Once shelled, store peas in perforated plastic bags in the refrigerator crisper for up to two days.

To shell peas, rinse the pods under cold running water. Snap off one end and pull it down the side, pulling the string along the back of the pod with it (pulling the string will "unlock" the pod's seal). Press the opposite side (where the pod is still sealed), open up the pod, and the peas will pop out. There is no need to rinse the peas before cooking.

Peas have wonderful affinities with cream sauces, butter, carrots, mustard, mint, dill, parsley, tarragon, sage, chervil, onions, mushrooms, potatoes, rice, ham, chicken, and shellfish.

COOKING TIMES
(times vary based on age and size of peas)

BOILING AND STEAMING: 4 to 10 minutes
MICROWAVING: 4 to 6 minutes
SAUTÉING AND STIR-FRYING: 5 to 7 minutes

SAUTÉED PEAS

PISELLI SALTATI IN PADELLA

An excellent side dish for meat and poultry. You may also stir the mixture into spaghetti or cooked rice for a complete, colorful meal. You may substitute frozen or canned peas for fresh. When using canned peas, drain and rinse under cold water before using, and reduce cooking time to 2 minutes.

4 tablespoons olive oil
2 pounds fresh peas
1 to 2 tablespoons water
½ cup chopped fresh parsley
Salt and freshly ground black pepper

HEAT the oil in a large skillet over low heat. Add the peas and water (to create steam), cover, and cook 3 to 5 minutes, until peas are just tender. Remove from the heat and stir in the parsley. Season to taste with salt and pepper and serve hot.

Serves 6

PEAS WITH HAM

PISELLI SALTATI CON PARMA COTTO

IF using canned peas, drain and rinse under cold running water. Drain and set aside.

In a large nonstick skillet, heat the oil over medium heat. Add the onion and sauté until golden. Add the ham and peas and cook until peas are tender (5 to 7 minutes for fresh, 1 to 2 minutes for canned).

2 pounds fresh or canned peas
2 tablespoons olive oil
1 small onion, minced
2 thick slices boiled ham, diced

Serves 6

PEAS WITH BACON

PISELLI AL BACON

2 pounds fresh or frozen peas,
    thawed

2 tablespoons unsalted butter

2 to 3 ounces bacon, finely chopped

Salt and freshly ground black pepper

I serve this dish with "sunny-side-up" fried eggs when preparing Sunday brunch for friends and family.

BLANCH the peas in a large pot of rapidly boiling water for 2 minutes. Drain and set aside. Melt the butter in a large skillet over medium heat. Add the bacon and sauté 5 minutes, until golden brown. Add the peas and sauté 2 to 3 minutes, until crisp-tender. Season to taste with salt and pepper and serve hot.

Serves 6 to 8

PEA SOUP

MINESTRINA CON PISELLI

I leave the peas whole in this recipe to create a light, broth-based soup. For a thicker soup, after seasoning with salt and pepper, puree half of the mixture in a blender and return puree to the pot.

5 cups vegetable stock or water, divided
2 cups fresh or frozen peas
1 tablespoon unsalted butter
1 tablespoon all-purpose flour
Salt and freshly ground black pepper

IN a large stockpot over medium-high heat, bring 4 cups of the stock to a boil. Add the peas and simmer 5 minutes.

Meanwhile, melt the butter and flour together in a small saucepan over medium heat, stirring constantly with a wire whisk. Cook until the flour is golden, stirring constantly. Gradually whisk in the remaining cup of stock and cook until the mixture thickens, stirring constantly with a wire whisk. Stir the mixture into the stockpot and simmer until the soup thickens and peas are tender, 3 to 5 minutes. Season to taste with salt and pepper and serve hot.

Serves 4

COUNTRY-STYLE PEAS

PISELLI ALLA CAMPAGNOLA

2 tablespoons unsalted butter

1½ cups small white onions, peeled
(or frozen and thawed)

1 pound fresh or frozen peas (see
Note)

2 medium potatoes (about
1½ pounds total), peeled and
cut into 1-inch cubes

3 carrots, peeled and sliced crosswise
into ¼-inch-thick rounds

1½ to 2 cups water or chicken stock

1 teaspoon salt

½ teaspoon freshly ground black
pepper

1 cup chopped fresh parsley

MELT the butter in a large saucepan over medium heat. Add the onions and sauté 3 to 5 minutes, until golden. Add the peas, potatoes, and carrots and sauté 5 minutes.

Add 1½ cups of the water, the salt, and pepper and bring to a boil. Reduce the heat, partially cover, and simmer 10 minutes, until peas and potatoes are tender, adding more water if necessary to prevent vegetables from sticking to pan.

Remove from heat, add the parsley, and toss to combine. Serve hot.

Serves 6 to 8

NOTE: *When using frozen peas, keep frozen until ready to use and, instead of adding with potatoes and carrots, add for the last 2 minutes of cooking time.*

RISOTTO WITH PEAS

RISOTTO CON PISELLI

IN a medium saucepan over medium heat, bring the stock to a simmer.

Meanwhile, heat the oil in a large saucepan over medium heat. Add the onion and sauté 3 to 5 minutes, until tender and golden. Add fresh peas, if using, and tomato and sauté 1 minute. Add the rice and salt and sauté 2 minutes, until rice is translucent.

Add ½ cup of the warm stock and simmer until liquid evaporates, stirring constantly with a wooden spoon. Add the remaining stock, 1 cup at a time, waiting until liquid is absorbed before adding next cup (risotto will take 18 to 20 minutes from the time the first liquid is added), stirring frequently.

Stir in the Parmigiano-Reggiano, thawed frozen peas, if using, and butter and simmer until cheese melts. Serve hot.

Serves 4

6 cups beef, chicken, or vegetable stock

2 tablespoons olive oil

1 small onion, finely chopped

2 cups fresh or frozen peas, thawed

1 beefsteak tomato, peeled, seeded, and diced

2 cups arborio (Italian short-grain) rice

½ teaspoon salt

1 cup freshly grated Parmigiano-Reggiano cheese

½ tablespoon unsalted butter

Peppers
PEPERONI

THERE ARE BASICALLY TWO TYPES OF PEPPERS—HOT AND SWEET. AS A GENERAL RULE, THE BIGGER THE PEPPER, THE MILDER AND SWEETER THE TASTE. THE SMALLER THE PEPPER, THE HOTTER IT WILL BE. AMONG THE SWEET PEPPERS, GREEN AND RED BELL PEPPERS ARE THE MOST POPULAR. THEY ARE ACTUALLY THE SAME VARIETY—RED PEPPERS ARE JUST

left on the vine long enough to fully mature. As green peppers ripen, their color changes and their flavor sweetens—yellow, orange, and purple bell peppers all start as green, and change colors as the peppers mature. Cubanelles, also know as Italian frying peppers, are not as sweet as bell peppers, but they add a refreshing "young" pepper taste to a variety of dishes (they are especially good when combined with other vegetables). The thick flesh of bell peppers makes them ideal for stuffing, while chopped peppers add wonderful sweet flavor and firm texture to soups, stews, salads, stir-fries, sauces, and casseroles.

There are so many hot pepper varieties that it would be nearly impossible to list them all. The most popular varieties include jalapeño, serrano, fresno, habanero, cayenne, Anaheim, and ancho or pablo chile (the words *pepper* and *chile* are used interchangeably).

Roasting peppers of any variety not only softens the crisp, juicy flesh but also mellows the raw taste and creates a wonderful smokiness. To roast peppers, blacken the skin by holding the pepper over the flame of a gas burner, or place pepper halves, skin side up, under the broiler. Once peppers are charred all over, transfer them to plastic or paper bags to steam (steaming loosens the skin). When cool enough to handle, remove the blackened skin and use the flesh as desired.

Fresh peppers are available throughout the year, with the season peaking August through September. When shopping, choose peppers with rich color and smooth skin that is free of bruises, scars, and wrinkles. Store uncut, fresh peppers in paper or perforated plastic bags in the refrigerator crisper up to one week. Cut peppers should be wrapped in plastic, refrigerated, and used within three days.

To prepare peppers for eating or cooking, use a sharp knife to cut around the stem at the top. Remove the top and pull out the core and seeds. Halve the peppers, remove additional seeds and membranes (the white portion), and slice as desired.

Bell peppers have natural affinities with rice, lamb, beef, poultry, onions, tomatoes, mild and sharp cheeses, pine nuts, saffron, parsley, marjoram, and oregano. Hot peppers can be used to add heat and flavor to virtually all savory dishes, and they have particular affinities with mild cheeses, green onions, cumin, chili powder, coriander, and cilantro.

PIEDMONT-STYLE PEPPERS

PEPERONI ALLA PIEMONTESE

3 yellow bell peppers, halved
    lengthwise and seeded

3 red bell peppers, halved lengthwise
    and seeded

4 whole anchovies, chopped

1 garlic clove

2 tablespoons olive oil

PREHEAT the broiler (see Note).
Place the pepper halves, skin side up, on a foil-lined baking sheet and press down to flatten. Place under the broiler and broil until blackened all over. Transfer the peppers to a plastic bag and let steam 5 minutes.

Remove the peppers from the bag and peel away and discard the blackened skins. Slice the peppers into strips and transfer to a shallow dish. Top with anchovies and the garlic clove. Pour over olive oil, cover with plastic wrap, and let stand 1 hour. Remove the garlic clove and serve at room temperature or chilled.

Serves 6 to 8

NOTE: *You may also blacken peppers by holding them over a flame until charred all over. Steam in a plastic or paper bag as directed, and peel away blackened skin.*

YELLOW PEPPERS IN THE OVEN

PEPERONI GIALLI COTTI AL FORNO

PREHEAT the broiler (see Note).

Place the pepper halves, skin side up, on a foil-lined baking sheet and press down to flatten. Place under the broiler and broil until blackened all over. Transfer the peppers to a plastic bag and let steam 5 minutes.

Preheat the oven to 400° F.

Remove the peppers from the bag and peel away and discard the blackened skins. Slice the peppers into thin strips and transfer to a shallow baking dish. Pour over 1 tablespoon of the oil and set aside.

In a small bowl, combine the remaining 2 tablespoons olive oil, the bread, olives, anchovies, capers, and black pepper to taste. Mix well and spoon mixture over peppers in baking dish. Bake 15 minutes, until topping is golden brown. Serve hot.

Serves 4 to 6

NOTE: *You may also blacken peppers by holding them over a flame until charred all over. Steam in a plastic or paper bag as directed, and peel away blackened skin.*

6 large yellow bell peppers, halved lengthwise and seeded

3 tablespoons olive oil, divided

1 slice bread, crust trimmed, center portion crumbled

3 black olives, sliced

2 whole anchovies, minced

1 tablespoon drained capers

Freshly ground black pepper

PEPPERS AND TOMATOES

PEPERONATA

6 ripe beefsteak tomatoes

2 to 3 tablespoons olive oil

4 red bell peppers, seeded and cut
    into thin strips

4 yellow bell peppers, seeded and cut
    into thin strips

2 green bell peppers, seeded and cut
    into thin strips

3 bay leaves

Salt and freshly ground black pepper

*This colorful blend of bell peppers and tomatoes makes a wonderful side
dish for roast chicken and grilled fish. I also like to spoon the mixture
over boiled rice and pasta.*

BRING a large pot of water to a boil. Cut large X's (just
enough to break the skin) on both ends of each tomato.
Immerse tomatoes in boiling water for 15 seconds. Remove
tomatoes with a slotted spoon and, when cool enough to handle,
peel away and discard outer skin. Halve the tomatoes, squeeze
out seeds, and chop into ¼-inch pieces. Set aside.

Heat the oil in a large skillet over medium heat. Add the
peppers and bay leaves and sauté 5 minutes, until peppers are
crisp-tender. Add the tomatoes and simmer until tomatoes have
broken down and sauce thickens, about 7 minutes. Remove from
the heat, discard the bay leaves, and season to taste with salt and
pepper. Serve hot.

Serves 6 to 8

TUNA STUFFED PEPPERS

PEPERONI RIPIENI CON TONNO

PREHEAT the oven to 400° F.
In a large bowl, combine the tuna, parsley, juice from both lemons, olive oil, salt, and pepper. Toss to combine.

Arrange the pepper halves in the bottom of a shallow roasting pan and spoon the tuna mixture into each pepper half. Bake 15 minutes, until peppers are crisp-tender. Remove from oven and serve warm.

Serves 4

2 6-ounce cans solid white tuna, drained

1 cup minced fresh parsley

2 lemons

2 to 3 tablespoons olive oil

1 teaspoon salt

½ teaspoon freshly ground black pepper

2 yellow bell peppers, halved lengthwise and seeded

2 red bell peppers, halved lengthwise and seeded

RAW PEPPER SALAD

INSALATA MISTA DI PEPERONI CRUDI

IN a large bowl, combine the bell peppers, tomatoes, and green and black olives.

Whisk together the oil and vinegar and season to taste with salt and pepper. Pour the mixture over the vegetables and toss to combine.

Serves 4 to 6

2 red bell peppers, seeded and cut julienne style

2 yellow bell peppers, seeded and cut julienne style

1 small green bell pepper, seeded and cut julienne style

2 medium plum tomatoes, sliced

3 green olives, pitted and halved

3 black olives, pitted and halved

1½ tablespoons olive oil

½ tablespoon vinegar

Salt and freshly ground black pepper

Potatoes

PATATE

THE POTATO, A RELATIVE OF TOBACCO AND THE TOMATO, IS THE WORLD'S LARGEST-SELLING VEGETABLE. CULTIVATED MORE THAN 4,000 YEARS AGO, POTATOES WERE A STAPLE FOOD OF THE INCAS. THE POTATO IS ACTUALLY THE SWOLLEN TIP OF AN UNDERGROUND STEM, AND IT STORES ENERGY IN THE FORM OF STARCH. THE ENERGY FROM THE

starch supports new stems that arise from the "eyes," small indents on the surface of the potato.

Market shelves are often brimming with potatoes day after day, so it's hard to believe there is just one crop per year. Thankfully, potatoes are harvested in various regions three out of the four seasons, so supply is uninterrupted year-

round. Fresh potatoes that are harvested and sold in the spring and summer are known as "new potatoes." They have a high moisture content and hold their shape after cooking, making them the best choice for potato salads, gratins, and stews. They are also a better choice for steaming and roasting. At the market, they are the smooth-skinned, round reds and whites, and oblong White Roses. The best way to tell if potatoes at the market are "new" is to rub the skin. If the skin comes off easily, it is a new potato. Potatoes harvested in the fall are put into cold storage, where they lose moisture. Since they are higher in starch, the flesh is dry and fluffy, perfect for frying, mashing, and baking. At the market, these are sold as russet or Idaho.

When shopping, select potatoes that are firm and heavy for their size, with taut, unblemished skin. Avoid greenish potatoes—they have been exposed to the sun and will have a bitter taste. Also avoid potatoes that have sprouted—they will be soft and bitter. Store unwashed, unwrapped potatoes in a cool, dark, dry place for up to one month. If you notice them sprouting, cut off the sprout and ¼ inch of the flesh beneath it.

To prepare potatoes for cooking, leave the skin on whenever possible—it contains much of the potato's nutrients and earthy flavor. When baking or microwaving whole potatoes, prick the surface all over with a fork or sharp knife to prevent potatoes from "exploding" owing to steam buildup. If you cut potatoes in advance, immerse them in cold water to prevent the flesh from becoming gray and discolored. And avoid cooking potatoes in aluminum or iron pots—both types of metals can darken the flesh.

Potatoes have natural affinities with butter, cream, mild and sharp cheeses, smoked meats, beans, peas, chives, green onions, round onions, mushrooms, garlic, parsley, rosemary, dill, basil, thyme, bay leaves, tarragon, and sage.

COOKING TIMES
(times vary based on whole potato size and width of potato slices)

BOILING AND STEAMING: 30 minutes for whole potatoes; 10 minutes for cut potatoes
BAKING AT 400° F: 45 to 60 minutes
MICROWAVING: 9 to 12 minutes
DEEP-FRYING IN OIL (OIL TEMPERATURE: 365° F): 2 to 3 minutes for French fries and 1-inch cubes; 3 to 5 minutes for larger pieces
SAUTÉING AND PAN-FRYING IN BUTTER OR OIL: 30 to 40 minutes for cubes and thin slices

POTATO SALAD

INSALATA DI PATATE

6 medium potatoes (about
   4½ pounds total), scrubbed

1 cup fresh parsley leaves, finely
   chopped

3 tablespoons olive oil

2 tablespoons white wine, or more to
   taste

Salt and freshly ground black pepper

PLACE the potatoes in a large stockpot and pour over enough cold water to cover. Set the pot over medium-high heat and bring the water to a boil. Reduce the heat to medium and cook 30 minutes, until potatoes are fork-tender. Drain and, when cool enough to handle, peel and cut into 2-inch chunks.

Transfer the potatoes to a large bowl, add the parsley, olive oil, and wine, and toss to combine. Season to taste with salt and pepper and serve warm or chilled.

Serves 6

 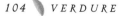

OVEN-ROASTED POTATOES
WITH FRESH ROSEMARY

PATATE ARROSTO AL FORNO CON ROSMARINO

When using very small (golf ball–size) potatoes, keep them whole for this dish. Cut larger red potatoes into 2-inch chunks before cooking.

PREHEAT the oven to 400° F.
Coat a large baking sheet with olive oil. Arrange the potatoes on top of the oil and sprinkle the top with rosemary and salt to taste.

Bake 50 to 60 minutes, until fork-tender. Serve hot or at room temperature.

Serves 6

4 to 5 tablespoons olive oil

2 pounds small red potatoes, scrubbed and quartered

2 to 3 fresh rosemary stems, leaves chopped (stems discarded)

Salt

Rosemary branches (fresh or dry)

POTATOES WITH PESTO

PATATE CON PESTO

4 medium potatoes (about 3 pounds total), scrubbed

½ cup plus 2 tablespoons olive oil, divided

1 cup packed fresh basil leaves

¼ cup pine nuts, lightly toasted (see Note)

¼ cup freshly grated Parmigiano-Reggiano cheese

½ teaspoon salt

¼ teaspoon freshly ground black pepper

Pesto is a specialty of Genoese cooking, and it is often paired with trinette or lasagna-style pastas. In this salad, the tangy pesto sauce coats warm, boiled potatoes. The result is a fresh and light potato salad that I like to serve with chilled meat platters. I often add fresh parsley leaves to enhance the bright green color of the sauce.

PLACE the potatoes in a large stockpot and pour over enough cold water to cover. Set the pot over medium-high heat and bring the water to a boil. Reduce the heat to medium and cook 30 minutes, until potatoes are fork-tender.

Drain the potatoes and, when cool enough to handle, peel and cut into 2-inch chunks. Transfer to a large bowl, add 2 tablespoons of the olive oil, and toss to coat.

Meanwhile, to make the pesto, in a blender combine the basil, pine nuts, Parmigiano-Reggiano, salt, and pepper. With the motor running, gradually add the remaining ½ cup of olive oil and process until smooth.

Add the prepared pesto to the potatoes and toss to coat (for the best results, toss potatoes with pesto while they're still warm).

Serves 4 to 6

NOTE: *Toast pine nuts by heating in a small skillet over medium heat 3 to 5 minutes, until golden, shaking the pan frequently.*

POTATO GRATIN WITH HAM

TIMBALLO DI PATATE CON PARMA COTTO

PREHEAT the oven to 375° F. Use 1 tablespoon of the butter to coat the bottom and sides of a 9x12-inch baking dish. Set aside.

Place the potatoes in a large stockpot and pour over enough cold water to cover. Set the pot over medium-high heat and bring the water to a boil. Reduce the heat to medium and cook 30 minutes, until potatoes are fork-tender.

Meanwhile, melt the remaining 4 tablespoons of butter in a small saucepan over medium-low heat. Add the flour and cook until the mixture becomes golden, stirring constantly with a wire whisk. Gradually whisk in the milk and simmer until the mixture is smooth and thick, about 3 minutes, stirring constantly with a wire whisk. Remove from heat.

Drain the potatoes and, when cool enough to handle, peel (if desired) and slice crosswise into thin slices. Arrange half of the potato slices in the bottom of the prepared baking dish. Top with half of the diced ham. Spoon over half of the milk mixture. Repeat the layers (potato slices, ham, milk mixture), using up remaining ingredients. Sprinkle the top with grated Parmigiano-Reggiano. Bake, uncovered, 45 minutes, until top is golden. Let stand 10 minutes before serving.

Serves 6

5 tablespoons unsalted butter, divided

4 medium potatoes (about 3 pounds total), scrubbed

4 tablespoons all-purpose flour

2 cups milk

1/2 pound baked ham, diced

1/2 cup freshly grated Parmigiano-Reggiano cheese

Radicchio

RADICCHIO

RADICCHIO IS THE ITALIAN NAME FOR CHICORY, AND THIS COLORFUL VEGETABLE HAS ALWAYS BEEN A WELCOME MEMBER OF THE EUROPEAN SALAD. THE BEAUTIFUL BURGUNDY LEAVES AND CONTRASTING WHITE RIBS MAKE IT A STRIKING ADDITION TO ANY PLATE. A RELATIVE OF ESCAROLE AND BELGIAN AND CURLY ENDIVE, RADICCHIO HAS SIMILAR qualities—firm leaves and a characteristic, refreshing bitterness.

Available year-round, radicchio is found either round or elongated, depending on the variety. The round variety, or *radicchio rosso,* is shaped like a small cabbage. The elongated Red Treviso variety has spear-shaped leaves. The leaves of the round variety are sturdy enough to act as edible "bowls" for a variety of salads, including those made with fruit, pasta, seafood, and poultry. They may also be used to hold dips and dressings for fresh fruits and vegetables. Both varieties are delicious raw and can be added to almost any mixed salad.

Cooking radicchio tames the bitterness and makes the vegetable an excellent partner for rich meat and game dishes. Both varieties of radicchio heads can be cut into wedges, brushed with olive oil, and grilled, roasted, and baked until golden brown and crisp-tender. Wedges may also be quickly sautéed and braised in wine or stock. The leaves may also be torn into pieces or cut into thin strips and sautéed with olive oil and fresh herbs. The mild bittersweet flavor of radicchio pairs well with olive oil; mild, sharp and spicy cheeses; smoked meats; hard-boiled eggs; mild and bitter greens; pine nuts; onions; carrots; olives; capers; white wine; vinegar; fruit; rosemary; basil; and parsley.

When shopping, look for fresh leaves with no browning around the edges or signs of wilting. The white core should be firm and unblemished. Stored in perforated plastic bags in the refrigerator crisper, radicchio will keep up to one week.

COOKING TIMES

BAKING AND ROASTING AT 350° TO 425° F
(WEDGES): 10 to 15 minutes

BRAISING (WEDGES): 7 to 10 minutes

SAUTÉING (TORN OR CUT LEAVES): 3 minutes;
(WEDGES): 2 to 3 minutes per side

GRILLING (WEDGES): 3 to 5 minutes per side

 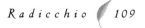

RADICCHIO ANTIPASTO

ANTIPASTO DI RADICCHIO

3 large eggs

1 cup fresh parsley leaves, finely chopped

2 tablespoons olive oil

2 tablespoons red or white wine vinegar

1 tablespoon drained capers

½ teaspoon salt

¼ teaspoon freshly ground black pepper

1 head radicchio (about ½ pound), leaves rinsed and patted dry

PLACE the eggs (in shells) in a medium saucepan and pour over enough cold water to cover. Set the pan over medium-high heat and bring the water to a boil. Lower the heat and simmer 14 minutes. Drain and plunge the eggs into ice water to prevent further cooking. When cool, remove the shells and cut the eggs into thin slices. Set aside.

In a medium bowl, combine the parsley, olive oil, vinegar, capers, salt, and pepper. Toss to combine.

Arrange the radicchio leaves on a serving platter and spoon over the parsley mixture. Top with the sliced eggs and serve at room temperature or chilled.

Serves 4

SAUTÉED RADICCHIO IN OLIVE OIL

RADICCHIO SALTATO CON OLIO D'OLIVA

BLANCH the radicchio leaves in a large pot of rapidly boiling water for 1 minute. Drain and set aside.

Heat the oil in a large skillet over medium heat. Add the radicchio leaves and sauté 2 minutes. Season to taste with salt and pepper and serve hot.

2 heads radicchio (about ½ pound each), leaves separated

2 to 3 tablespoons olive oil

Salt and freshly ground black pepper

Serves 4

MIXED SALAD OF RADICCHIO, BELGIAN ENDIVE, AND BOSTON LETTUCE

INSALATA MISTA DI RADICCHIO CON BELGA E LATTUGA

WASH the leaves of the radicchio, endive, and Boston lettuce and pat dry. Transfer the leaves to a large serving bowl and set aside.

In a small bowl, whisk together the oil and vinegar and season to taste with salt and pepper. Pour the dressing over the leaves and toss to coat.

1 large head radicchio, leaves separated

2 bunches Belgian endive, leaves separated

1 head Boston lettuce, leaves separated

1½ tablespoons olive oil

½ tablespoon vinegar

Salt and freshly ground black pepper

Serves 6

 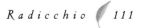

RADICCHIO SOUP

ZUPPA DI RADICCHIO

5 cups lightly salted water

1 large head radicchio, leaves cut into 2 pieces

1½ tablespoons olive oil, divided

3 bread slices, diced

Salt and freshly ground black pepper

BRING the water to a boil in a large stockpot over medium-high heat. Add the radicchio and cook 2 minutes. Reduce the heat to medium-low, add ½ tablespoon of the olive oil, and simmer 10 minutes.

Meanwhile, heat the remaining tablespoon of olive oil in a large nonstick skillet over medium-high heat. Add the bread and sauté 3 to 5 minutes, until golden brown on all sides. Remove from the heat.

Season the soup with salt and pepper to taste, ladle into bowls, and serve with bread on the side.

Serves 4

Spinach

SPINACI

There are two types of spinach sold at the market—smooth and curly. The difference is obvious not only in the shape of the leaves but also the stems; the curly variety has noticeably bigger stems. There is no difference in taste, however, so always choose the spinach with the freshest-looking leaves.

Spinach is available year-round, but the season peaks during the cool temperatures of spring and fall (spinach production is lowest during the hot summer months). At the market, spinach can be sold in bunches, as loose leaves, or prewashed and packaged in plastic bags. Baby spinach is also readily available, and since the stems are thin and the leaves are small, it is excellent eaten raw.

Whatever form of spinach you choose, always select crisp, fresh leaves, and avoid any leaves with blemishes, soft spots, wilting, or yellowing. All spinach (including the prewashed variety) is notoriously dirty and sandy, so be sure to rinse the leaves well before using. Although best used the day of purchase, fresh spinach will keep in paper or perforated plastic bags in the refrigerator crisper up to two days.

Spinach can be eaten raw or cooked and has great affinities with butter, olive oil, cream, mild and sharp cheeses, lemon, vinegar, pine nuts, hard-boiled eggs, pastry, garlic, onions, mushrooms, smoked meats, anchovies, seafood and shellfish, walnuts, pine nuts, almonds, dried fruit, parsley, oregano, dill, and nutmeg.

To prepare spinach for cooking, wash the leaves thoroughly in fresh, cold water to remove all sand and dirt. Trim the stems at the base of the leaves (use the stems to flavor soups and stocks). Use the leaves whole, tear them into smaller pieces, or stack the leaves and cut them into thin strips, called chiffonade.

COOKING TIMES

BOILING: 1 to 2 minutes

STEAMING: 3 to 4 minutes

MICROWAVING: 5 to 7 minutes

SAUTÉING: 3 to 5 minutes

BABY SPINACH SALAD

INSALATA DI SPINACI FRESCHI

This fresh salad is excellent topped with slices of hard-boiled eggs. Add dressing just before serving, to prevent spinach leaves from wilting.

½ cup fresh lemon juice

2 to 3 tablespoons olive oil

½ teaspoon salt

¼ teaspoon freshly ground black pepper

1 pound fresh baby spinach, rinsed well and patted dry

IN a small bowl, whisk together the lemon juice, olive oil, salt, and pepper.

Transfer the spinach to a large bowl, pour over the lemon dressing, and toss to coat.

Serves 6

SAUTÉED SPINACH IN OLIVE OIL

SPINACI SALTATI ALL'OLIO D'OLIVA

I prefer to use medium spinach leaves (not baby spinach) for this dish.

2 pounds fresh spinach, stems trimmed

3 to 4 tablespoons olive oil, or more as necessary

1 whole garlic clove, peeled

Salt and freshly ground black pepper

WASH the spinach leaves several times in fresh cold water to remove all dirt and sand.

Blanch the spinach in a large pot of lightly salted, rapidly boiling water for 2 minutes. Drain and set aside.

Heat the oil in a large skillet over medium-high heat. Add the garlic and blanched spinach and sauté 5 minutes. Discard the garlic. Season to taste with salt and pepper and serve hot. This salad can be topped by thin slices of Parmigiano-Reggiano.

Serves 4

PUREED SPINACH

PURE' DI SPINACI

3 pounds fresh spinach leaves
   (medium-sized leaves, not baby
   spinach)

3 tablespoons unsalted butter

Salt and freshly ground black pepper

WASH the spinach leaves several times in fresh cold water to remove all dirt and sand. Remove the stems.

Blanch the spinach in a large pot of lightly salted, rapidly boiling water for 2 minutes. Drain and transfer to a food processor fitted with the metal blade. Process until finely chopped.

Transfer the spinach to a large skillet and set the pan over medium heat. Cook 5 minutes, until hot. Add the butter and cook 2 minutes, until butter melts. Season to taste with salt and pepper and serve hot.

Serves 4 to 6

SPINACH MOLD

SFORMATO DI SPINACI

Sliced hard-boiled eggs or tomatoes make a beautiful garnish on top of this dish.

3 pounds fresh spinach (medium-sized leaves), stems trimmed

6 tablespoons unsalted butter, divided

¼ cup all-purpose flour

2 cups milk

2 large eggs

⅓ cup freshly grated Parmigiano-Reggiano cheese

Salt and freshly ground black pepper

1 tablespoon dry bread crumbs

PREHEAT the oven to 350° F.
Wash the spinach leaves several times in fresh cold water to remove all dirt and sand.

Blanch the spinach in a large pot of lightly salted, rapidly boiling water for 2 minutes. Drain the spinach and finely chop. Transfer to a large bowl, add 2 tablespoons of the butter, and toss until butter melts. Set aside.

Melt the remaining 4 tablespoons of butter in a small saucepan over medium-low heat. Add the flour and cook until the mixture becomes golden, stirring constantly with a wire whisk. Gradually whisk in the milk and simmer until the mixture is smooth and thick, about 3 minutes, stirring constantly with a wire whisk. Remove from heat and pour the mixture over the spinach. Add the eggs, Parmigiano-Reggiano cheese, and salt and pepper to taste. Mix well.

Lightly butter a tube pan and sprinkle the bread crumbs into the bottom of the pan. Pour the mixture into the prepared pan.

Bake 45 minutes to 1 hour, until the top is golden and a wooden pick inserted near the center comes out clean. Turn it out onto a serving platter and serve hot.

Serves 4 to 6

SPINACH FRITTATA

FRITTATA DI SPINACI

3 pounds fresh spinach (medium-sized leaves), stems trimmed, or 3 10-ounce packages frozen spinach, thawed and dried

5 tablespoons olive oil, divided

12 large eggs, lightly beaten

½ cup freshly grated Parmigiano-Reggiano cheese

Salt and freshly ground black pepper

4 to 5 fresh basil leaves, chopped

During the hot summer months, this is one of my favorite cold dishes. I often bring this frittata when we sail on Long Island Sound; the combination of flavors and scenery takes me back to the Mediterranean. You may use fresh or frozen spinach for this dish. Using fresh will yield a more delicate flavor.

WASH the fresh spinach leaves several times in fresh cold water to remove all dirt and sand.

Heat 3 tablespoons of the oil in a large skillet over medium-high heat. Add the spinach and sauté 3 to 5 minutes, until the leaves are wilted and the liquid evaporates. Remove from the heat, transfer to a cutting board, and finely mince. Set aside.

In a large bowl, whisk together the eggs, Parmigiano-Reggiano, and salt and pepper to taste. Add the sautéed spinach and basil and mix well.

Heat the remaining 2 tablespoons of oil in a large skillet over medium heat. Add the egg mixture and cook 3 minutes, until set and almost cooked through to the top. Gently shake the skillet—if it feels firm and the top is not liquid, the bottom is done.

Invert the frittata onto a large plate and slide the frittata back into the skillet, uncooked side down. Place the skillet over medium heat and cook 1 minute, until cooked through (a wooden pick inserted near the center will come out clean). Serve warm or chilled.

Serves 6

String Beans

FAGIOLINI

STRING BEANS ARE SLENDER AND BRIGHT GREEN, COMMONLY REFERRED TO AS SNAP OR GREEN BEANS. THE TERM "STRING BEANS" ORIGINALLY REFERRED TO A TOUGH STRING THAT RAN THE LENGTH OF THE BEAN, A STRING THAT MAY OR MAY NOT BE FOUND IN MODERN VARIETIES. WHEN SHOPPING, SELECT BEANS THAT ARE SMALL, TENDER, AND FIRM.

They should be so fresh they "snap" when broken in half. Particularly thin and tender beans are often labeled as *haricot verts,* and are usually more expensive. Avoid large, pale beans with swollen pods and big, developed seeds—they are past their prime, less sweet, and likely to be tough and fibrous. Fresh beans will keep up to one week in perforated plastic bags in the refrigerator crisper.

Fresh beans should be cooked until just tender, not wilted. Cooking times vary according to age and variety, but in rapidly boiling water, cooking time is about 2 minutes. To keep the bright green color, in room temperature or cold dishes, run just-cooked beans under very cold water—this halts the cooking process. String beans may also be braised, and this method works especially well for older beans since it sweetens and tenderizes them.

String beans have great affinities with olive oil, olives, butter, eggs, tomatoes, vinegar, lemons, nuts, dill, mint, chervil, and parsley.

STRING BEAN SALAD
WITH HARD-BOILED EGGS

INSALATA DI FAGIOLINI CON UOVA SODE

THIS is a great cool salad for a hot summer luncheon. Blanch the beans in a large pot of rapidly boiling water for 2 minutes. Drain and rinse immediately under cold water to stop the cooking. Drain and transfer to a large salad bowl.

Whisk together the olive oil and vinegar. Season to taste with salt and pepper and pour the mixture over the beans. Toss to coat. Top beans with hard-boiled eggs and serve at room temperature or chilled.

Serves 4 to 6

1½ pounds fresh string beans, ends trimmed and strings removed

3 tablespoons olive oil

1½ tablespoons vinegar

Salt and freshly ground black pepper

4 hard-boiled eggs, chilled and quartered

STRING BEAN SALAD

FAGIOLINI IN INSALATA

1½ pounds fresh string beans, ends trimmed and strings removed

10 black olives, pitted and sliced

2 tablespoons olive oil

1 tablespoon vinegar

Salt and freshly ground black pepper

BLANCH the string beans in a large pot of rapidly boiling water for 2 minutes. Drain and rinse immediately under cold running water to stop the cooking. Drain and transfer to a large salad bowl. Top with olives.

Whisk together the oil and vinegar. Season to taste with salt and pepper and pour the mixture over the beans and olives. Toss to coat. Serve at room temperature or chilled.

Serves 4

SAUTÉED STRING BEANS WITH TOMATO SAUCE

FAGIOLINI SALTATI CON SALSA DI POMODORO

1½ pounds fresh string beans, ends trimmed and strings removed

2 tablespoons olive oil

2 cups Tomato Sauce (page 132)

Salt and freshly ground black pepper

BLANCH the string beans in a large pot of rapidly boiling water for 2 minutes. Drain and set aside.

Heat the oil in a large nonstick skillet over medium heat. Add the beans and Tomato Sauce and simmer 2 minutes to heat through. Season to taste with salt and pepper and serve hot.

Serves 4

 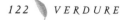

RUSSIAN SALAD

INSALATA RUSSA

I don't know why this is called "Russian Salad," but it's one of my favorites (maybe because so many vegetables are all tossed together!). You may add salt and pepper to the mayonnaise as desired, but I prefer my mayonnaise without pepper.

IN a large pot of rapidly boiling water, blanch the peas, string beans, carrots, broccoli, cauliflower, and bell peppers for 3 minutes. Drain, transfer to a large bowl and add the tomatoes and olives. Set aside to cool while you prepare the mayonnaise.

Place the yolks in a large bowl, food processor, or blender. With the motor running (or while using a wire whisk), beat in 2 tablespoons of the olive oil. Gradually beat in the lemon juice. Season to taste with salt. Add the remaining 4 tablespoons olive oil, 1 tablespoon at a time, and beat or whisk until the mixture forms a thick consistency. If desired, season to taste with pepper.

Pour the mayonnaise over the vegetables and toss to coat. Cover with plastic and refrigerate at least 1 hour.

Transfer salad to a large serving dish and garnish with hard-boiled eggs and parsley or basil.

Serves 4 to 6

1 pound fresh peas

String beans, about ¼ pound, ends trimmed and strings removed

2 small carrots, peeled and cut into chunks

3 to 4 broccoli florets

3 to 4 cauliflower florets

1 red bell pepper, seeded and cut into chunks

1 yellow bell pepper, seeded and cut into chunks

2 small tomatoes, cut into chunks

3 green olives, halved

MAYONNAISE

8 large egg yolks

6 tablespoons olive oil, or more as desired

2 to 3 tablespoons fresh lemon juice

Salt and freshly ground black pepper (optional)

2 hard-boiled eggs, thinly sliced, for garnish

Fresh parsley or basil, for garnish

Tomatoes

POMODORI

LTHOUGH IT SEEMS THERE ARE COUNTLESS TOMATO VARIETIES AT THE MARKET, THEY ACTUALLY GROW IN JUST TWO SHAPES— ROUND AND PLUM, OR PEAR‹SHAPED. CHERRY TOMATOES ARE USUALLY THE FIRST ROUND TOMATOES OF THE SEASON, AND THEY CAN BE RED, GOLD, ORANGE, OR YELLOWISH GREEN. THESE SWEET, JUICY TOMATOES are excellent raw, and they add flavor and color to any salad or mixed‹vegetable dish. The next size up—the small‹ and medium‹size tomatoes— are moderately juicy and perfect for slicing and adding to sandwiches, salads, and chilled side dishes. The larger tomatoes, also known as "beefsteak," are rich and meaty (yet still juicy), and they can be used both raw and cooked.

Plum and pear‹shaped tomatoes are oval or teardrop‹shaped and they range in size from small to medium. Often referred to as "roma" tomatoes, their flesh is thick and somewhat dry, making them ideal for sauces, soups, stews, gratins, and any other cooked tomato dish. But plum toma‹

toes, with a tangy-sweet flavor, also add a distinct freshness to warm salads and uncooked sauces.

Larger tomatoes are now available in colors ranging from red to green to yellow, gold, and orange. Green tomatoes are typically crisp and tart, while yellow and orange tomatoes are profoundly sweet and fruity.

Tomatoes are available year-round, but peak season lasts from midsummer until the first frost. Tomatoes that are grown out of season are raised in greenhouses or hydroponically (in water rather than soil). Since tomatoes continue to ripen off the vine, many commercially available varieties are picked before they are fully mature. Unfortunately, color develops as they ripen but flavor does not. "Vine-ripened" tomatoes are often the most flavorful because they are left on the vine long enough to show most of their mature color.

When shopping for fresh tomatoes it helps to use your nose; if it smells like a ripe tomato, it probably is. Select full-colored, ripe but firm tomatoes that are free of bruises and soft spots. They should be heavy for their size and, if leaves are attached, they should be moist and fresh looking. Store tomatoes unwrapped at room temperature, where they will soften if unripe in about two days. Soft tomatoes that are past their prime for salads and sandwiches are often ideal for soups and stews.

When a recipe calls for peeled and seeded tomatoes, cut large X's (just enough to break the skin) on the bottom of each tomato and immerse them in rapidly boiling water for 15 seconds. Remove the tomatoes with a slotted spoon and, when cool enough to handle, peel away and discard the skin. Halve the tomatoes crosswise and squeeze out the seeds. Use as desired.

Tomatoes pair beautifully with butter, olive oil, cream sauces, mild and sharp cheeses, onions, garlic, rice, seafood and shellfish, cucumbers, peppers, eggplant, dried beans, fresh peas, zucchini, eggs, bread, potatoes, olives, capers, basil, oregano, thyme, dill, tarragon, and parsley.

FRESH TOMATO SALAD

INSALATA DI POMODORI FRESCHI

4 beefsteak tomatoes (about 2 pounds
  total), thinly sliced

3 tablespoons olive oil

1 tablespoon balsamic vinegar

½ teaspoon salt

¼ teaspoon freshly ground black
  pepper

3 or 4 fresh basil leaves

ARRANGE the tomato slices on a serving platter. In a small bowl, combine the olive oil, vinegar, salt, and pepper. Mix well and pour the mixture over the tomatoes. Arrange the basil leaves over the top.

Serve at room temperature or chilled (for the best results, remove from refrigerator 30 minutes before serving).

Serves 4

FRESH TOMATOES WITH MOZZARELLA AND BASIL

POMODORI FRESCHI CON MOZZARELLA E BASILICO

Fresh mozzarella is ideal for this dish. Select premium mozzarella (a cow's-milk cheese sold fresh, often in a liquid bath) for its creamy center and fresh milk flavor. Buffalo mozzarella, made from the milk of water buffaloes, may also be used. For a delightful presentation, alternate slices of tomatoes and mozzarella in concentric rings on a serving platter before topping with basil and olive oil.

½ pound fresh mozzarella cheese, sliced into ¼-inch-thick slices

4 to 5 ripe beefsteak tomatoes, rinsed and patted dry

8 fresh basil leaves

2 tablespoons olive oil, or more as desired

Salt and freshly ground black pepper

ARRANGE the mozzarella slices on a serving platter (when using a round platter, arrange slices in a circle around the outside, creating a flower shape).

Slice the tomatoes crosswise into ¼-inch-thick slices and place each slice on a slice of mozzarella. Place the basil leaves in the center of the platter and sprinkle the olive oil over the dish. Season to taste with salt and pepper and serve at room temperature.

Serves 6 to 8

RAW TOMATOES STUFFED
WITH SALSA VERDE

POMODORI CRUDI RIPIENI DI SALSINA VERDE

A delicious side dish for a summer luncheon.

1 round loaf (about ½ pound)
  sourdough bread (pagnotta di
  pane)

1 cup fresh parsley leaves, chopped

3 whole anchovies, finely chopped

1 tablespoon drained capers

3 tablespoons olive oil

2 tablespoons red wine vinegar

½ teaspoon salt

5 large beefsteak tomatoes, halved
  crosswise and cored, pulp and
  seeds removed

CUT the bread into 1-inch cubes and transfer to a large bowl (see Note). Set aside.

In a small bowl, combine the parsley, anchovies, capers, olive oil, vinegar, and salt. Mix well and pour the mixture over the bread. Toss to combine and let stand 20 minutes.

Spoon the bread mixture into the hollowed-out tomato halves and serve room temperature or chilled.

Serves 8 to 10

NOTE: *I prefer to use the soft, crustless, inside portion of the bread. You may prepare this dish with or without the crust.*

RAW TOMATOES
STUFFED WITH TUNA

POMODORI CRUDI RIPIENI DI TONNO

USING a sharp knife, cut large X's (just enough to break the skin) on bottom of each tomato. Immerse the tomatoes in rapidly boiling water for 15 seconds. Remove tomatoes from boiling water with a slotted spoon and, when cool enough to handle, peel away and discard skins. Immerse the tomatoes in an ice water bath to refresh.

Drain the tomatoes and slice ½ inch off each top, making a "lid." Make tomato "shells" by scooping out the seeds and flesh from each half. Turn the shells and lids upside down to dry.

Meanwhile, in a large bowl, combine the tuna, eggs, parsley, the juice from two of the lemons, the olive oil, and capers. Mash all ingredients together with a fork until well blended and season to taste with salt and pepper.

Spoon the mixture into the tomato shells and transfer the stuffed tomatoes to a serving plate. Slice the remaining lemon into thin slices and arrange around tomatoes as a decorative garnish.

Serves 4

4 large beefsteak tomatoes

2 6-ounce cans tuna in water, drained

4 hard-boiled eggs, chopped

½ cup fresh parsley, finely chopped

3 lemons

3 tablespoons olive oil, or more as needed

2 tablespoons drained capers

Salt and freshly ground black pepper

TOMATOES WITH POTATOES
AND STRING BEANS

POMODORI CON PATATE E FAGIOLINI

3 medium potatoes (about 2 pounds
total), peeled and cut into 2-inch
pieces

3 tablespoons olive oil

2 pounds fresh string beans, ends
trimmed and strings removed

4 medium beefsteak tomatoes, cut
into 2-inch pieces

4 or 5 Sicilian black olives, finely
chopped

Salt and freshly ground black pepper

BLANCH the potatoes in a large pot of rapidly boiling
water for 5 minutes. Blanch the string beans also. Drain
and set aside.

Heat the oil in a large skillet over medium heat. Add the
blanched potatoes, string beans, tomatoes, and olives and sauté
until the potatoes are golden, the string beans are crisp-tender,
and the tomatoes are broken down, 10 to 15 minutes. Season to
taste with salt and pepper and serve hot.

Serves 6 to 8

ENGLISH MUFFIN PIZZETTE

PIZZETTE CON ENGLISH MUFFIN

*When my children were young, we had tea together when they returned
from school. I didn't want to feed them cookies, so I served this special
pizzette. Serve the pizzettes with drinks or tea, garnished with
fresh basil leaves.*

4 *English muffins, split*

2 *medium tomatoes, sliced*

Salt

4 *slices mozzarella or Brie cheese*

Olive oil

1 *tablespoon dried oregano or*
12 fresh oregano leaves, or
3 leaves fresh basil, minced

PREHEAT the oven to 250° F.
Warm the English muffins in the oven until soft, about 5
minutes. Remove from the oven and preheat the broiler.

Top each English muffin half with a tomato slice and sprinkle tomatoes with salt. Place the cheese on top of the tomatoes
and drizzle with olive oil and oregano or basil.

Place the pizzettes on a baking sheet and put under the
broiler. Broil until the cheese melts and turns golden brown.

Serves 4

TOMATO SAUCE

SALSA DI POMODORO

1½ tablespoons olive oil

½ medium onion, finely chopped

1 pound fresh plum tomatoes,
chopped

3 fresh basil leaves, minced, or
2 tablespoons dried oregano

Salt and freshly ground black pepper

*An excellent topping for sautéed string beans (page 122). This robust,
hearty sauce may also be used to add flavor and color to pasta, grilled
chicken, steamed and grilled fish, and steamed and sautéed vegetables
(such as broccoli, asparagus, cauliflower, and fresh beans).
Another way I cook tomato sauce: no onions, 1 peeled tomato sautéed
in olive oil, salt and pepper and basil (fresh) or dried oregano—
simple and delicious!*

HEAT the oil in a large skillet over medium heat. Add the
onion and sauté until golden brown, 3 to 5 minutes.

Add the tomatoes and cook 5 to 8 minutes, until tomatoes
are broken down and sauce thickens (do not overcook).

Add the basil or dried oregano and season to taste with salt
and pepper.

Makes 2 cups

Zucchini

ZUCCHINE

ALSO KNOWN AS SUMMER SQUASH, ZUCCHINI ARE THIN, YELLOW AND DARK GREEN VEGETABLES THAT ARE TYPICALLY 6 TO 8 INCHES LONG (SIZE MAY VARY DEPENDING ON THE FARMER—SOME ZUCCHINI ARE QUITE FAT). THE TERM "SUMMER" REFERS TO A TIME WHEN ZUCCHINI WAS AVAILABLE ONLY DURING THE WARMER MONTHS OF THE YEAR.

Thanks to improvements in agriculture and refrigeration, zucchini are now available year-round. Zucchini and yellow squash are harvested before they reach full maturity, so the soft skin and buttery flesh are both edible.

When shopping, select firm (not hard), shiny vegetables that are heavy for their size. Avoid vegetables with soft spots, cuts, or other blemishes. The best-tasting zucchini and yellow squash are no more than 6 inches long and 2 inches wide. Many Italian cooks believe zucchini is "past its prime" if the blossom is no longer attached. If you can find zucchini with a blossom, great, but they are often difficult to find.

Fresh zucchini has sweet-tasting flesh, while "old" vegetables can be somewhat bitter. Store zucchini and yellow squash in perforated plastic bags in the refrigerator crisper up to five days.

Zucchini is excellent served raw; simply prepare it as you would a cucumber (unpeeled), sliced into matchsticks or thin rounds. To prepare zucchini for cooking, rinse the skin to remove soil, trim the ends, and use as desired. To preserve flavor and texture, cook zucchini very quickly in a small amount of liquid or olive oil.

Zucchini has affinities with other summer flavors, such as tomatoes, onions, sweet and hot peppers, corn, garlic, oregano, basil, parsley, and dill. The vegetable also pairs well with sharp cheese (especially feta and Parmigiano-Reggiano), sage, rosemary, lemon, and olives.

COOKING TIMES
(times vary based on size of slices)

BOILING, MICROWAVING, AND SAUTÉING: 2 to 4 minutes

STEAMING: 4 to 6 minutes

DEEP-FRYING IN OIL (OIL TEMPERATURE: 365° F): 2 to 3 minutes for ¼-inch-thick slices

BAKING AT 350° F (IN GRATINS WITH CREAM, BUTTER, AND CHEESE AND IN CASSEROLE DISHES WITH OTHER VEGETABLES): 25 to 30 minutes for ½-inch-thick slices and 1-inch cubes

SAUTÉED ZUCCHINI
WITH OLIVE OIL AND PARSLEY

ZUCCHINE TRIFOLATE CON
OLIO D'OLIVA E PREZZEMOLO

*I prefer to sauté the zucchini with a whole garlic clove that is later
discarded. That way, the garlic imparts its distinct essence without
overpowering the delicate flavor of the zucchini.*

4 tablespoons olive oil

3 zucchini (about ½ pound each),
   rinsed and cut crosswise into
   ¼-inch-thick rounds

1 whole garlic clove

2 tablespoons finely chopped parsley,
   or more as desired

3 tablespoons white wine vinegar

Salt and freshly ground black pepper

HEAT the oil in a large skillet over medium heat. Add the
zucchini and garlic and sauté 5 minutes, until the zucchini
rounds are tender and golden. Remove from the heat and
remove the garlic.

Add the parsley and vinegar and toss to combine. Season to
taste with salt and pepper and serve hot.

Serves 4

RAW ZUCCHINI SALAD
WITH OLIVE OIL AND LEMON

ZUCCHINE CRUDE IN INSALATA
CON OLIO D'OLIVA E LIMONE

20 baby zucchini, rinsed and sliced
   crosswise into ¼-inch-thick
   rounds

3 tablespoons extra virgin olive oil

1 to 2 lemons

Salt and freshly ground black pepper

Use baby zucchini for this recipe, found in "Petit Gourmet" packages.

IN a large bowl, combine the zucchini rounds, olive oil, and the juice from one or both lemons. Toss to combine.

Season to taste with salt and pepper and serve at room temperature or chilled.

Serves 6

RAW ZUCCHINI SALAD
WITH PARMIGIANO-REGGIANO

INSALATA DE ZUCCHINE CRUDE
CON PARMIGIANO-REGGIANO

Be sure to use baby zucchini for this wonderful salad—a perfect lunch side dish on a hot summer day.

USING a sharp knife, mandoline, or food processor, cut the zucchini crosswise into paper-thin slices. Arrange the slices on a serving plate in slightly overlapping concentric rings (to form a wheel shape).

In a small bowl or jar, combine the olive oil, the juice from the lemons, and salt and pepper to taste. Whisk together or shake jar until blended. Pour the mixture over the zucchini.

Just before serving, top zucchini with cheese slices.

Serves 2

3 small (baby) zucchini
3 tablespoons olive oil
2 to 3 lemons
Salt and freshly ground black pepper
16 thin slices Parmigiano-Reggiano cheese

FRIED ZUCCHINI

ZUCCHINE FRITTE

3 cups olive oil

4 zucchini (about 1/2 pound each),
   rinsed and cut crosswise into
   1/2-inch-thick rounds

3 large eggs, lightly beaten

1/2 cup all-purpose flour

Salt and freshly ground black pepper

1 to 2 lemons, sliced

This dish is best served warm, with lemon squeezed over the top.

HEAT the olive oil in a heavy stockpot until a thermometer reads 350° to 375° F.

Dip the zucchini rounds into the beaten eggs and turn to coat. Dip the rounds into the flour, turn to coat both sides, and shake off excess flour.

Add the zucchini to the hot oil in batches (to keep oil temperature constant) and fry until golden brown, 2 to 3 minutes per side. Remove with a slotted spoon, transfer to paper toweling, and sprinkle with salt and pepper to taste.

Arrange the fried zucchini on a serving platter and garnish with lemon slices. Serve hot.

Serves 4 to 6

STUFFED ZUCCHINI

ZUCCHINE RIPIENE

Excellent served warm or chilled.

6 medium zucchini

2 tablespoons olive oil

1 medium onion, minced

1 medium carrot, peeled and minced

10 to 12 ounces ground veal

½ cup chopped fresh parsley

Salt and freshly ground black pepper

PREHEAT the oven to 400° F.

Blanch the zucchini in a large pot of rapidly boiling water for 2 minutes. Drain and set aside.

Meanwhile, heat the oil in a large skillet over medium heat. Add the onion and carrot and sauté until golden brown, 3 to 5 minutes. Add the veal and increase the temperature to medium/high and cook 2 minutes. Reduce the heat to low and simmer 5 minutes. Add the parsley and season to taste with salt and pepper. Remove from the heat.

Slice the zucchini lengthwise into two halves and remove the seeds from each half, forming "boats." Stuff the veal mixture into the zucchini halves and transfer the stuffed zucchini to a shallow baking dish.

Bake 20 minutes, until tops are golden brown. Serve warm or refrigerate until ready to serve.

Serves 6

ZUCCHINI SOUP WITH CROUTONS

ZUPPA DI ZUCCHINE CON CROSTINI

2 pounds zucchini, cut into chunks

2 cups chicken or vegetable broth

1½ tablespoons olive oil, divided

1 tablespoon chopped fresh rosemary

Salt and freshly ground black pepper

2 slices bread (preferably day-old),
   cut into cubes

2 tablespoons freshly grated
   Parmigiano-Reggiano cheese

BLANCH the zucchini in a large pot of rapidly boiling water for 4 minutes, until tender. Drain the zucchini and transfer to a blender. Add the broth and 1 tablespoon of the olive oil. Puree until smooth. Season to taste with rosemary and salt and pepper to taste.

Heat the remaining ½ tablespoon olive oil in a large nonstick skillet over medium heat. Add the bread cubes and cook 2 to 3 minutes, until golden brown on all sides.

Just before serving, reheat the zucchini soup in a medium saucepan over medium-low heat. Ladle into bowls and serve hot with croutons and Parmigiano-Reggiano on the side.

Serves 4

Index

Conversion Chart *Equivalent Imperial and Metric Measurements*

American cooks use standard containers, the 8-ounce cup and a tablespoon that takes exactly 16 level fillings to fill that cup level. Measuring by cup makes it very difficult to give weight equivalents, as a cup of densely packed butter will weigh considerably more than a cup of flour. The easiest way therefore to deal with cup measurements in recipes is to take the amount by volume rather than by weight. Thus the equation reads:

1 cup = 240 ml = 8 fl. oz.   ½ cup = 120 ml = 4 fl. oz.

It is possible to buy a set of American cup measures in major stores around the world.

In the States, butter is often measured in sticks. One stick is the equivalent of 8 tablespoons. One tablespoon of butter is therefore the equivalent to ½ ounce/15 grams.

LIQUID MEASURES

Fluid Ounces	U.S.	Imperial	Milliliters
	1 teaspoon	1 teaspoon	5
¼	2 teaspoons	1 dessertspoon	10
½	1 tablespoon	1 tablespoon	14
1	2 tablespoons	2 tablespoons	28
2	¼ cup	4 tablespoons	56
4	½ cup		110
5		¼ pint or 1 gill	140
6	¾ cup		170
8	1 cup		225
9			250, ¼ liter
10	1¼ cups	½ pint	280
12	1½ cups		340
15		¾ pint	420
16	2 cups		450
18	2¼ cups		500, ½ liter
20	2½ cups	1 pint	560
24	3 cups		675
25		1¼ pints	700
27	3½ cups		750
30	3¾ cups	1½ pints	840
32	4 cups or 1 quart		900
35		1¾ pints	980
36	4½ cups		1000, 1 liter
40	5 cups	2 pints or 1 quart	1120

SOLID MEASURES

U.S. and Imperial Measures		Metric Measures	
Ounces	Pounds	Grams	Kilos
1		28	
2		56	
3½		100	
4	¼	112	
5		140	
6		168	
8	½	225	
9		250	¼
12	¾	340	
16	1	450	
18		500	½
20	1¼	560	
24	1½	675	
27		750	¾
28	1¾	780	
32	2	900	
36	2¼	1000	1
40	2½	1100	
48	3	1350	
54		1500	1½

OVEN TEMPERATURE EQUIVALENTS

Fahrenheit	Celsius	Gas Mark	Description
225	110	¼	Cool
250	130	½	
275	140	1	Very Slow
300	150	2	
325	170	3	Slow
350	180	4	Moderate
375	190	5	
400	200	6	Moderately Hot
425	220	7	Fairly Hot
450	230	8	Hot
475	240	9	Very Hot
500	250	10	Extremely Hot

Any broiling recipes can be used with the grill of the oven, but beware of high-temperature grills.

EQUIVALENTS FOR INGREDIENTS

all-purpose flour—plain flour
baking sheet—oven tray
buttermilk—ordinary milk
cheesecloth—muslin
coarse salt—kitchen salt
cornstarch—cornflour

eggplant—aubergine
granulated sugar—caster sugar
half and half—12% fat milk
heavy cream—double cream
light cream—single cream
parchment paper—greaseproof paper

plastic wrap—cling film
scallion—spring onion
shortening—white fat
unbleached flour—strong, white flour
zest—rind
zucchini—courgettes or marrow